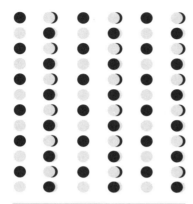

Broadway's Fabulous Fifties

How the Playmakers Made It Happen

Arthur Miller

Howard Lindsay

Russel Crouse

Abe Burrows

Moss Hart

Elia Kazan

Joshua Logan

Paddy Chayefsky

Joseph Kramm

Howard Bay

Mary Drayton

D1714048

**Edited by
The New Dramatists
Alumni Publications
Committee**

HEINEMANN ◑ **Portsmouth, NH**

Heinemann
A division of Reed Elsevier Inc.
361 Hanover Street
Portsmouth, NH 03801–3912
www.heinemanndrama.com

Offices and agents throughout the world

This book was compiled and edited by the New Dramatists Alumni Publications Committee: John von Hartz, chair; Louis C. Adelman, Anna Marie Barlow, Charles Best,
Bonnie Bluh, and Joel Wyman.

Library of Congress Cataloging-in-Publication Data
Broadway's fabulous fifties : how the playmakers made it happen / compiled and edited
by the New Dramatists Publications Committee: John von Hartz . . . [et al.].
    p.   cm.
    ISBN 0-325-00425-0 (pbk. : acid-free paper)
    1. American drama—20th century—History and criticism.   2. Theater—New
York (State)—New York—History—20th century.   3. Broadway (New York,
N.Y.)—History.   4. Playwriting.   I. Von Hartz, John.   II. New Dramatists, Inc.
Publications Committee.

PS351 .B69 2002
822'.91409—dc21

                                                                      2001007489

Editor: Lisa A. Barnett
Production: Lynne Reed
Cover design: Joni Doherty
Typesetter: Kim Arney Mulcahy
Manufacturing: Steve Bernier

Printed in the United States of America on acid-free paper
06   05   04   03   02   VP   1   2   3   4   5

Cast of Characters
In Order of Their Appearance

A typical New Dramatists craft discussion. The guest is Lillian Hellman (extreme left), author of *The Little Foxes* and many other distinguished plays. To the right of Miss Hellman are Howard Lindsay, moderator, and Michaela O'Harra, founder of the New Dramatists.

Acknowledgments

We wish to extend our appreciation to the following for their help:

Present and former members of the New Dramatists staff: Todd London, Karen Noyes, Joel K. Ruark, Jana Jevnikar, and Paul Alexander Slee.

New Dramatists alumni: Mark Druck, Harding Lemay, Quincy Long, and interns Sam Forman and Claudia Breitman.

Our agent, Donald Maass.

Especially to Michaela O'Harra, the founder of the New Dramatists, without whom these craft discussions would not have been held.

Introduction

They were memorable evenings, full of humor, warmth, and wisdom. On one occasion, a young theater hopeful asked the consummate craftsman Howard Lindsay to define what was dramatic. Lindsay shot back, "Two hungry dogs with one juicy bone between them."

Memory serves up another incident. New Dramatists guest George Abbott, director and playwright, was asked to comment on *pace*. Mr. Abbott (no one ever called him George) was famous for his dexterous staging of farces. Pace in a play, said the master of the genre, is not the result of actors furiously running in and out and slamming doors. Pace is determined by the script, how many times during the course of the play the protagonist undergoes a reversal of fortune, and how much stage time passes between those reversals.

One evening the question was raised whether it was worth tolerating a gifted but egotistical, trouble-brewing actor in a company, or if it was better to push for his replacement. The person who passed judgment has, regrettably, been forgotten. But the words of that old pro are still remembered: "I'll take a talented bastard every time."

These evenings, at which experienced professionals came to the New Dramatists and shared what they knew about the theater, were called *craft discussions*. Over the years, they were a regular part of New Dramatists activity. Only ten of these evenings were recorded in the 1950s. (Unfortunately, the session with Mr. Abbott was not one of them.)

This volume contains the edited transcripts of those ten. The words of the participants have not been changed. Repetitions and references to persons now obscure and events long irrelevant have, however, been deleted. If you "listen" as you read, you will hear the voices of the greatest artists of the day—Howard Lindsay, Arthur Miller, Moss Hart, Elia Kazan, and others—speaking from hard-won experience. Their words constitute a unique manual for making great theater.

How did these discussions and the New Dramatists come about? Broadway boomed after World War II and into the 1950s. Musicals such as *My Fair Lady* and *Guys and Dolls* had America laughing and singing songs that soared not only from the stage but as popular hits performed on radio and television, in nightclubs, and on jukeboxes. The dramatic scene was graced by such American masters as Arthur Miller and Tennessee Williams. The final play of Eugene O'Neill, *Long Day's Journey into Night*, burst onto the stage in 1956, affirming once again, albeit posthumously, his gigantic talent.

The dream of creating a hit on Broadway was not lost on the nation's playwrights. They flocked to New York, scripts or ideas for plays in hand. But the theater world was limited in scope and accessibility and could not assimilate them all. Competition for agents, minor productions, even readings became intense. At one meeting of the Dramatists Guild, members and associate members jammed into the Alvin Theater to express their frustration at their inability to have their work produced, or even heard.

One immensely successful man of the theater stood before the angry writers and soothed the crowd with his calm and reasonable approach. He was Howard Lindsay—playwright, director, and producer. Many of those present were impressed by his professional demeanor. Among them was Michaela O'Harra, a young writer whose play had recently been taken on the road, then closed without explanation. Ms. O'Harra later wrote, "I had very definite ideas about what could be done for new playwrights, but the possibility that anyone with clout would be willing to listen to them had never occurred to me. So I went home, composed a 'dream scheme' incorporating the whole complex of ideas, dubbed it a

Plan for Playwrights and wrote the man a letter." The man, of course, was Howard Lindsay.

To Ms. O'Harra's joy and to the everlasting benefit of the theater, Mr. Lindsay was won over by the plan. He and Ms. O'Harra became a vital force in creating the organization that implemented it—the New Dramatists. In effect, the plan introduced a selected number of playwrights with modest credits to the intimate world of Broadway theater through a series of steps.

The craft discussions were an important part of the New Dramatists program. The organization also sponsored regular panel discussions, where members would read and critique a colleague's script; rehearsed readings, in which a cast of professional actors read a play aloud for the playwright's benefit, followed by a critique session; and workshops, in which a fully rehearsed play was presented at the New Dramatists to a live audience. In the organization's production observerships, Broadway impresarios permitted a New Dramatist to be present at script, casting, and production conferences, and during all rehearsal and out-of-town tryouts for a new Broadway-bound play. Through the generosity of management, the New Dramatists offered free theater admissions that made it possible for members to be guests at a stream of incoming plays.

All this began modestly. A storage closet at the Hudson Theatre, then owned by Mr. Lindsay and Russel Crouse, was converted into an office with a desk and a phone. Members gathered around a large table in the theater's greenroom for meetings and craft discussions. Mr. Lindsay rounded up support from Moss Hart, Richard Rodgers, Oscar Hammerstein II, Maxwell Anderson, John Golden, Russel Crouse, Elmer Rice, and John Wharton. With Mr. Lindsay and Ms. O'Harra, they became the New Dramatists Committee and gave the fledgling organization a governing body with a formal structure. Michaela O'Harra took on the job of Executive Director.

When the Hudson was sold, the organization moved to the Empire Theater. When that theater changed hands, the City Center offered office space on the second floor and additional space for rehearsals and readings. But after a few years, the City Center reclaimed the space and the New Dramatists had to make do with a small, rundown location off the Bowery.

But then fortune smiled. By chance, a board member, actress June Havoc, overheard two janitors at the Actors Studio talking about a former church at 424 West 44th Street that was empty and for sale. Through the generosity of the John Golden Fund, it became the New Dramatists' permanent home.

Since its formation in 1949, more than five hundred men and women have been New Dramatists. Of these, ten won the Pulitzer Prize, twenty received the Tony Award, fifty won Obie Awards, the Drama Desk Award went to seventeen, and nine took home the Susan Smith Blackburn Award.

Over the years, Ms. O'Harra's original plan for playwrights has been modified and supplemented. The development of musicals is being served by a composer-librettists studio. Workshops and readings of new musicals and operas are now available. A national and international playwright exchange now involves several American cities and foreign countries. A summer Lake Placid residency for members began in 1995.

The New Dramatists now administer significant awards, prizes, and fellowships. *Scriptshare* makes members' plays available to eighteen producing organizations that pay to subscribe. A *Plays and Playwrights* catalog is published annually. A bulletin, *In the Works,* is distributed monthly. Internship and volunteer programs have been instituted to assist in many activities.

If the theater professionals represented in this book could see the active, productive community that is thriving on West 44th Street, we believe they would be pleased. They contributed much to the professional growth of the playwrights with whom they spent these memorable evenings. Their thoughts, experiences, and wisdom still play a part in fulfilling the New Dramatists' purpose of nurturing and furthering the development of the American playwright. And they can still provide knowledge and pleasure to all who love the theater.

—The Editors

PHOTOGRAPH BY PARRY STUDIO.

Howard Lindsay

(1889–1968)

He knew theater. As an actor, he played vaudeville, tent shows, burlesque, silent pictures, and repertory, where he also worked as stage manager. Not to mention the directing, producing, writing, and play doctoring he did. Howard Lindsay could clearly explain everything about plays—their construction, casting, and presentation—and pepper his lessons with humorous and insightful anecdotes. As a result, his mentorship was acknowledged by scores of writers, actors, and directors.

Mr. Lindsay left Harvard for the American Academy of Dramatic Arts. Returning after U.S. Army infantry service in World War I, he displayed his versatility by acting, directing, and writing. He collaborated on his first play in 1927. When Lindsay and Russel Crouse met in 1934, they began a lifelong theatrical partnership. One of their greatest successes—and certainly the most endearing—was *Life with Father*, which was based on the memoirs of Clarence Day. It opened in 1939 and became Broadway's longest running non-musical. Mr. Lindsay starred in the original cast, playing Father opposite his wife, the actress Dorothy Stickney.

Lindsay and Crouse garnered a Pulitzer Prize for their drama about politics, *State of the Union* (1945). As producers, they mounted *Arsenic and Old Lace* (1941), John Patrick's *The Hasty Heart* (1945), and Sidney Kingsley's *Detective Story* (1949) before turning their attention to creating the book for musicals such as Irving Berlin's *Call Me Madam* (1950) and *The Sound of Music* (1959), with music by Richard Rodgers.

Mr. Lindsay endeared himself to playwrights then and for years to come by aiding, supporting, and backing Michaela O'Harra in forming the New Dramatists in 1949. He gave his time and his energy to the organization, creating a board of directors with some of the most prestigious names in the theater and working tirelessly to help lesser-known writers have a place where they could learn their craft. Indeed, if ever a person gave himself to the theater, it was Howard Lindsay.

A New Dramatists Craft Discussion
with Howard Lindsay
January 1956

MR. LINDSAY: I have some notes here. You know that book that you think you're going to write and have made notes for? I looked through them and what I could understand of the notes I brought down with me.

I was speaking to an artist recently, a very good artist, Walt Kuhn, and he was telling me about some students who studied painting under him. One of them came to him after a couple of years and said, "Mr. Kuhn, when am I going to learn everything there is about painting?" Kuhn said, "Never. I don't know everything. If I did, I would stop painting probably, because it would bore me." Nobody knows all there is to know about playwriting, nor can ever learn in a lifetime all there is.

We do, as we go along through the years, practicing in front of audiences, learn a little. We get the feel of certain things, and that is about the only way you really can learn deeply about playwriting. I came into the theater through the stage door, and all I know is what I learned in the theater. But, through thirty years or more, I have come to certain conclusions and made certain observations, and those I shall try to talk about with you.

Everything I am going to say here today should be prefaced by this: "As a rule." There are no rules in the theater that you can't break, except the rule against boring an audience. If you do break them, you must be breaking them deliberately, with full knowledge that you are running a risk, and you had better be sure you can write very far above the average before you do break them.

The theater is a very humbling game. That is what the Scotsman said about golf. I suppose the only people who know all there is to know about the theater are dramatists or directors after their first success. As the dramatist and play director go on, they find out they do not know it all. They find out another distressing thing, which is that they make the same mistakes again and again. You say, "Why did I do that? I should have known better." It is a curious matter.

What I have to say here is not going to be very well organized, but it is going to fall into these three basic categories: first, the organization of the emotions of the audience; second, story progress; third, dramatization.

The first job of the playwright is to organize the emotions of the audience, in favor of certain characters. Then you increase that emotion that you have organized by getting those characters into trouble. It's the amount of trouble that they're in, multiplied by the affection that the audience has for those characters, that gives you that product—emotion.

Years ago I used to go to wrestling matches. Here is what happened: A man in green tights and a man in black tights would get into the ring. They would make a few tentative passes at each other, trying a few holds, seemingly testing the other man's strength and skill. Then, fairly early in the match, the fellow in the green tights would suddenly kick the other man with his feet and hit him in the face, and the crowd would yell, "Why, the dirty dog. The dirty dog."

They had organized the emotions of the audience. They had a hero and a villain immediately. Then the man in the black tights, the hero, would look hurt and indignant and go after the other man, still using fair play, and the crowd would roar and hope that he would throw the fellow in the green tights for a loss, and it would look as though he might, for a moment. But then the man in the green tights would go after the other fellow and he would again abuse him and give him the knee, and the crowd would get very indignant and angry.

Toward the end of it, the man in the green tights would have the other man at his mercy. He would be hitting and kicking him, and the crowd would get angrier and angrier. It looked as though there would be no chance whatever for the fellow in the black tights to survive. But at the last second he would suddenly come to life, throw the man in the green tights around, get him down and pin his shoulders to the floor, and the crowd would go mad. The reason for the crowd to be excited was that their emotions had been organized. They were stirred in favor of one of the opponents.

It's good to have charming and witty dialogue; lots of plays have succeeded without it. Good characterization is fine, very helpful; lots of plays have succeeded without it. But they do not succeed unless they organize the emotions of the audience, keep that story moving forward and make it really happen in front of the audience. In the organization of emotions, is it more important to show the people you're going to *like* first, and then the ones you're going to *dislike?* Will the audience respond favorably if you present the person to be *disliked* first? It would be absolutely impossible to lay down a rule about that. That would differ with every play. By the end of the first act the audience should know who they like and who they don't like.

A manager named William Harris Jr. gave me a play and said, "It needs rewriting; see what you think." I read it and was very attracted by it, but not enough to want to stop to rewrite it because I was busy with something else. Several years later, another man sent for me and said, "I've got a play here that I think is pretty good, but it isn't right yet. Will you read it?" It was the same play. I read it and I was attracted to the material, and yet I knew it wasn't a good play. At first I didn't know why. Then I read it again, studied it, and I suddenly realized why it wasn't. There were two very attractive people in it, a man and a woman. They were never in trouble once. Who was in trouble at the end of the second act? All the people you didn't like. That's what was wrong with it.

Now, some plays have succeeded in doing the reverse of what I've just told you, but very few, and they have to be extraordinarily well written. Don't expect to reward an audience by defeating someone they hate.

It's my theory that everyone has to write one play about a bitch. They think they're going to succeed in making audiences hate this woman so much that when she gets her comeuppance in the last act, that'll sell tickets. It won't sell tickets. Not unless you can write as well as Lillian Hellman or Tennessee Williams.

QUESTION: Even though you dislike them, aren't those characters sympathetic?

MR. LINDSAY: No.

QUESTION: In something like *The Little Foxes*? Isn't Regina sympathetic?

MR. LINDSAY: That's the kind of play I'm telling you not to write. Hellman can get away with it because she writes so damn well. The only characters I thought were sympathetic in that play were the daughter, the husband, and poor Birdie. I liked them. No, I didn't care for Regina. She was an exciting character to spend an evening with in a way, because she was so well written and quite a gal.

QUESTION: There is a struggle between two sides, a dramatic situation. So on that basis, it becomes possible for the audience to choose sides.

MR. LINDSAY: I'm glad they could choose sides and there was a struggle, but I did not say anything about conflict when I mentioned dramatization. The basis of dramatization is the conflict between different forces. Now, it can be between people, it can be between a villain and a hero, it can be between two or three people here and three or four people there, it can be inside the person themselves. But there has to be that conflict for dramatization.

You come to the theater to hear a story told in terms of acting. An audience wants to be emotionally interested in the characters of your story. That is a demand that has never changed from the first time an audience met to hear a story. Around the campfires outside of the caves there must have been a fellow who could tell a pretty good story. At one time or another, a listener said, "Why don't we get together and get him to tell a story?" That was the first time any audience ever met deliberately for the purpose of hearing a story. They made that demand upon the teller of that story, that they wanted to be emotionally interested in some character he was telling about, emotionally interested in favor of that character. *And they wanted a reward for their emotions.*

I am only talking about New York theater. That is the only theater I know anything about. It is the feeling with which they leave that theater that is going to send them out to tell their friends to be sure to see that play or to stay away from it. That is the test. If we send them out only to tell their friends, "Don't go to see it," or "*I* liked it," and nothing else, we fail. It is the feeling, the satisfaction, the emotional reward with which these people leave the theater, that is the test. I saw a sentence in a review recently about a play. The writer said, "It didn't add up to a rewarding evening in the theater."

The reward can come one of two ways: either through the satisfaction of having the character they are interested in emotionally, sympathetically, win out over circumstances, or other people; or he must be tragically defeated. But if he is tragically defeated, their reward must be a depth of pity and compassion that is satisfying. There is great satisfaction in a depth of pity and compassion. We feel a little better when they have been deeply aroused. But if you are going to write a play in which the emotional sympathies of the audience are defeated, it has to be really a spiritual experience.

Good God, frustration is one of the most unhappy experiences in our lives. To ask people to spend their evening to get them emotionally interested in some character or characters and then to frustrate that emotion—why the devil would you think they would want to spend their time and money to go through that experience? They wouldn't. They will resent it.

Sam Harris [a producer] was one of our really great men of the theater; not an articulate man, not a man of academic background, but a man with a sure sense of the business. He was the one who created the phrase "Who am I rooting for?" That is what he wanted to know, "Who am I rooting for?" because he knew the audience wanted to root for somebody.

You have to seduce the audience's emotions in favor of a character or set of characters. Then you get those characters into trouble. That comes under the head of dramatization. Here is a phrase I got out of a Burns Mantle review: He spoke of "sympathetic emotional compensations." That says in three words all that I have been talking about since I started. That is the most basic thing in playwriting.

That presumes, of course, that when you start writing your play you know how it is going to end. Somebody said to George Kaufman, "I wish you would look at this and see what is wrong with the third act," and George said, "I can tell you now. Your first." What he meant was that the fellow didn't know where he was going when he started. I get pretty impatient at these scripts with good first acts and good second acts, but in which the author hasn't got any third act because he didn't know where he was going. Your last five minutes are the most terrifically important five minutes in your play because those are the five minutes just before the audience goes out and makes up its mind as to how much it likes that play.

Bill Maguire started writing a play some years ago which never came to town, and the trouble with that play was he didn't know where he was going when he started. The play was around a situation between two women. The husband had given up his career to be with his wife so that she could have her career. Then the husband got fed up with it and met another woman. Bill could end the play either way, send him back to his wife or keep him with the other woman. The mistake was in not knowing which woman was going to win out before he wrote the play.

Don't start a play unless you know what your emotional sympathetic compensations are going to be. We work like the devil on a play and then take it out of town. Then we find there are two things that can lick us: One is that the audience doesn't believe it, and the other is that they don't care. Not caring is what I'm talking about. If the audience does not care about the people or what happened to them, you haven't any play. They must care.

There are certain mathematics to playwriting. The emotional compensations at the end of the play are in ratio to two elements, the depths of the audience's affection for the sympathetic characters and the depth of the trouble that those people get into, and either overcome or are overcome by. Those two things, the depth of the audience's affection for the sympathetic characters multiplied by the depth of their trouble, equal the audience's emotional reward.

You have created in the audience an emotional interest for a certain character. Then you excite the audience. You threaten their emotions because you threaten your character by putting him up against circumstances or other people, so that it looks as though he is going to be in some way defeated or hurt. The audience should be very frightened about what is going to happen to that character. When the character overcomes the circumstances, then comes the warmth of the audience's satisfaction. The amount of that warmth is the product of their affections multiplied by their fears.

Here is a note phrased a little academically: "The easiest threat against the audience's emotional sympathies is against something they agree is to be held precious." We all know how we fight for life. We fight to keep alive when we are desperately ill. Everybody does. So, if you threaten a character with death, you have a pretty good threat. Here's another: We still are a romantic race. We still believe—thank God—that the consummation of love is a very desirable and precious thing. So, if you have threatened them with the loss of that consummation, you have a pretty good threat. We have a pretty good threat today to the liberty of the individual. The turmoil that the world is going through today is a threat that we can take very seriously.

I saw a picture called *Mr. Deeds Goes to Town* some years ago. The authors uncovered a pretty good one there. They threatened to send

Gary Cooper to an insane asylum. That was a real threat. We knew he was sane. He was a little bit more sane, perhaps, than the rest of the world. But he was a very kind and generous person, and that made some people suspicious of him and other people had other reasons for wanting him declared insane. So they put Gary Cooper on trial before a lunacy commission, and naturally everybody was very excited by it.

You can go back through the history of drama and you can find out what audiences deemed precious. Take *Antigone*. You remember, the funeral rites for her brother. The Greek audiences agreed that was something to worry about, and that was the basis of the tragedy. In *Richelieu*, when he threatened to launch the "curse of Rome," that was a great threat.

If you are going to depart from threatening a character with the loss of something that the audience agrees is to be held precious, then you have to increase the depth of their sympathy toward that character, and you have to write better. The audience has to be much more fond of that character in order to see him wanting to win something which the audience as a whole does not think is tragically important in their own lives.

To go back to the emotional setup of an audience: The feelings of audiences will change with the changing times. Be conscious of how your audience is feeling. Several years ago, Bob Sherwood wrote a play called *Idiot's Delight*. It was a play that told what a useless, terrible thing war was. Let's have no more of it. That is what the audience felt at that time. Then came Mr. Hitler, Mr. Mussolini, and they made an attack upon the things we held precious. We knew we had to fight, our pacifism went by the board, and Mr. Sherwood wrote *There Shall Be No Night*.

Your plays must reflect the emotions of your audience of the day, of the week, of the hour almost, that you produce your play. So, when you are thinking about arousing your audience's emotions and threatening them with the defeat of those emotions, you have to give thought to how an audience is feeling as of today.

QUESTION: You mentioned that emotion is basic in the theater. And that something that's intellectual is another thing. Is there a meeting ground?

MR. LINDSAY: Oh, yes. I don't mean that you have to disregard the mind entirely. The purpose of the theater is not to confirm the mind, it's to confirm the emotions, or convince the emotions. You can make an audience applaud something that most of the very people applauding would not applaud as *individuals*. You can get an audience very excited about, say, the little lame girl that gets up and walks in the last act. It's a lot of tommyrot, of course. But you can get the audience excited by it. As soon as they get out from under the influence of the play, however, they know that it's not what they feel or think at all. You see, an audience is quite different from an individual.

In an audience, you're sitting next to strangers, and your reactions are qualified by that. Somebody on the stage tells a very, very dirty joke. It might be a joke that as an individual you would laugh your head off at. But, with this strange lady next to you, or strange gentleman, you're not going to. Or, they might get out some platitude about freedom of speech or something else that people would applaud. But when you get out, you realize the argument wasn't sound. You might have applauded yourself, because everyone else was and you're not going to let them think you don't agree that the American flag is one of the most wonderful things in the world, by God! But when you get out of the theater, you say, "Why, dammit, what they did was meretricious; we shouldn't have applauded that, a lot of hooey!"

I once heard a friend, in speaking of a play, say, "If I don't care any more than that, it has to be funnier." That means this: I have talked to you about, and laid great emphasis upon, the organization of the emotions of the audience. I have told you how deep they have to be. Well, you may say they are not deep in a farce. Of course not. That does not mean they shouldn't be organized, that the audience mustn't be in favor of certain characters or a character. But there is a great variance as to the depth.

Now we have gotten around to story progress. The speed of the progress of your story has to have a direct relationship to the depth of the emotional response. The more shallow is the emotional response, the more swiftly does your story have to pass given points. The farce has to move faster than the drama. If the emotional response is deep, your play can have a leisurely pace, but as your emotional response gets less deep, then the swifter must be the progress of your story. Think of story points as telegraph poles that you are passing on a train. In the farce you have to pass those poles quickly. The story has to keep going forward all the time. Your scenes are very much shorter. You are jumping from one situation to another, to another, to another, to another. There always has to be that compensation to the audience when the emotions of the audience are not engaged so deeply.

Years ago, I staged a couple of plays of Booth Tarkington's. Tarkington wrote some very fine plays. He also wrote a lot of other plays, not all of them successful. The critics used to complain they were thin. Well, each play I staged was so charming, so amusing, you couldn't cut a line. Tarkington could write so well that he could write ten pages to a scene that should have taken only three. If he had only been able to write three then he would have had a swifter story and more story.

I think William James pointed out the difficulty of concentration. He pointed out that if a person took an object such as a table, and determined to keep his mind upon that table, he could only do so until he had exhausted everything there was to notice about that table. He must be continually finding something new about that table. The minute he exhausted new things to observe, he cannot keep his mind on it any longer. The same with a scene. As soon as the members of the audience have exhausted everything new in that scene, they cannot keep their minds on it.

Don't write your scene beyond its point. When you are through with a scene, you are through with it. This is a trick I learned from [playwright] Owen Davis. Get into your next scene as quickly as you can, in two lines if you can. Sometimes we take two or three pages to get from one scene to the next scene. That is all waste stuff. Your story has to be continuously moving forward.

Don't make your scenes too long. When we tried out *Life with Father* out of town, we thought if we could get through the first act and into the second, it would be all right. We didn't expect anything of the first act, but if we could get into the second act, we would be safe. We were very surprised on the opening night because the first act went like a house afire. We were very jubilant. We said, "Now we are all right." When we got to the second act it didn't go nearly as well. It was way under par. When we began to examine why, after looking at it for a week and studying the script, the reason was very obvious: Every scene was a little too long. We had to take two lines out of that scene, four out of that scene, and six out of that. Every scene being a little too long, it slowed the play up. Just a couple of lines makes it too long. Four lines makes it very much too long, and six are impossible. By merely cutting in the second act, it was improved tremendously.

One thing that will give pace to your story progress is giving your leading character or characters a destination. Have them on their way somewhere; wanting to achieve this, wanting to achieve that. If they have that behind them, if they are on their way somewhere, you will get more scenes as the story progresses.

Get your big laughs closer together if you are writing comedy. Don't be afraid to cut out small laughs. Keep those big laughs as close together as you can. There is another flaw in scripts which is not uncommon. Take the kind of scene in a play where the lady used to have a dream. The second act would be a dream. When she wakes up, the story is no further ahead than when she went to sleep. Any time you put something in a play so that at the end of a scene your personal story is no further ahead than when you began, that is not good playwriting.

Everything must happen in front of an audience. They must learn about the characters, not by somebody telling them what a sweet girl Suzie is, and being expected to fall in love with Suzie because somebody says so. No, she's got to *be* attractive, and she's got to *win* that audience. If the father likes liquor, don't have somebody *tell* the audience, *show* it to them. That's the motto of an audience: they're all from Missouri; they say, "Show me!" You have to dramatize your play, which is a quite different thing from narrating it. You have to dramatize by continually creating the incidents so that something is exciting.

Keep in front of an audience the people that they like to spend their time with. If you have disagreeable people to help you with your story, get them on, let them help you, and get them off. Keep the people the audience likes to spend its time with in front of it. Don't keep in front of the audience people it doesn't like unless they are really entertaining. Of course, if they are too entertaining, the audience may get to like them. That is a danger.

Now, I have gotten around to the second thing that we find about a play out of town that licks us. There are two things: The audience doesn't care or the audience doesn't believe us. When we are out of town, we can always fix up the first act, we can always fix up the second act, we can always fix the third act, but when they don't care or don't believe it, then we are licked.

Now, as to conviction. I think the greatest reward for audiences while they are watching a play is conviction. When an audience sits there and forgets it is seeing a play, when it is just believing what is happening on a stage, that is the greatest pleasure you can give an audience. You can get conviction in two ways, one with sheer veracity, one where your writing and acting is so true that they do believe in it as it goes along. The other way, or an added way, I might say, is where you create a will to believe by being entertaining.

Brooks Atkinson [the *New York Times* critic] was trying to analyze why he didn't like the play *Reap the Harvest*. He said he supposed it was because he didn't believe in it. He spoke about a clock that didn't move, an automobile horn that didn't sound anything like an automobile horn, and a woman in the play calling upon a character to help her move a table which she could have moved herself, but it seems they had to get another character on the scene.

It is true that if you like the play you do not quarrel with those things. We know the minute we bore an audience, they begin to question. When they are bored, their eyes look around the set, and they say, "Good God, that chandelier shouldn't be that high." Well, we have to hang chandeliers high so that the people in the gallery can see the people on the stage. If there is a clock on the stage, they look at it and see that its hands haven't moved in the last half hour. They hear an automobile effect, and say it doesn't sound like an automobile. If they are interested and being entertained, they don't make those observations.

If you are going to write a farce, get as much conviction as you can early. You can't start on a broad basis and then get narrower. You can't start with farcical comedy, and then end with light comedy. Be careful when you are writing a farce or melodrama. Convince them as much as you can. We have to do that today. I am not talking now about such a play as Thornton Wilder's *The Skin of Our Teeth*. I am talking about the ordinary rules of playwriting. I am warning you, if you are going to break these principles, write as well as Thornton Wilder writes.

I used to read a lot of plays, and I would come across this astonishing flaw in playwriting, a flaw easily made. The playwright gets the wrong characters into trouble. Now, there is no point in threatening a character that the audience doesn't like, because it is not emotionally involved with him. Threaten the fortunes of the characters they do like. Those are the people to get into trouble. For the purpose of dramatization, when you are getting your sympathetic characters into trouble, have that trouble as desperate as you can. You are not going to threaten them with their lives if you are writing a light comedy or a high comedy. But make the trouble as desperate as you can within the key of your play. Remember, the audience's satisfaction at the end of the play is in ratio to the desperateness of the situation from which your characters have escaped.

Make your exposition pay its own way. The first act is the hardest act to write, the hardest to act and the hardest to stage, because we are pushing so many facts across to the audience. They are not yet acquainted with relationships. In the first act you have to be giving the audience that information. It has to pay its own way either in humor or in excitement. The characters just can't sit down and say, "As you know, my dear Gaston, this is the year 1793, and *la belle France* is torn with internal dissension." Don't do it through discussion. Do it through incident which will reveal to the audience what you want revealed. They should not be conscious at the end of the first act that you have told them all these things about your characters, and they won't be conscious of it if what they are seeing on the stage is interesting, exciting, or amusing. If the customers think a scene is being played for its own sake, they are not conscious of the fact that you are telling them all these things you have to tell them.

Owen Davis said he always distinguished between plot and story: *story* was the story of the leading characters and their relationship with each other and with the people around them. *Plot* was the incidents, the things that *happened* that changed their relationship to each other or to the people around them, things that affected them. Plot was the incident.

Now, I staged a play of Davis' years ago, and after opening in Cincinnati and reading the notices, Davis said, "Well, they like the story, but they don't believe the plot. I'll change the plot." I didn't know his definitions at that time. He said, "I'll tell you what, Howard. I won't come to the theater tonight. I'll stay at the hotel and change the plot. Bring the four principal people down after the performance, and I'll have the new stuff for them." I looked at him aghast, and I said, "Mr. Davis, do you mean you're going to change the plot while we're playing the play at the theater this evening?" He said, "Yes, that won't be difficult."

I brought the leading people down to the hotel that night, and Davis had the plot changed. He said, "Now, on page three, change these two lines. On page six, here are four lines. Now, there's a new page twenty-two," etc., and he went right through the play. Now, I don't mean it was a terrific change and I don't remember exactly.

The play went like this: Frank Conroy was a young man in the employ of Frederick Burt. Frank was a brilliant designer and an engineer. He had contributed many valuable ideas that Burt had patented. Now, Burt was planning to marry a very pretty young girl. The mother of the young girl thought that he was interested in her at first but it turned out to be her daughter. So, she was forcing her daughter into marriage with Burt, and the daughter happened to be in love with the young man [Conroy], and at the end of the play eloped with him. But, the things that happened—Conroy's discovering that he had no rights in the inventions, no right to the profits, that he could be fired right out of the firm and he would be if he interfered in the older man's love affair— it was something about this that strained the credulity of the audience, Mr. Davis thought, and in one night he changed it.

He hadn't changed the story one iota. The relations between the characters were absolutely the same, the antagonism between the boy and the girl at certain points, the antagonism between the boy and the employer, the mother's attitude toward the employer and the daughter. Everything that had to do with human relationships remained exactly as it was. He had changed the things that precipitated the situations. There was a scene which revealed the fact that the young man was in love with the girl and, very late in the play, there was a scene that the girl was in love with the boy. It was the things that precipitated those revelations that Davis had changed.

So when anybody asks you to rewrite your play, ask yourself, "Are they asking me to change my play or are they asking me to change my plot?" They are two separate things.

Now, a plot has to be in key with your story. You can't suddenly, in the middle of a light story of a boy's and a girl's love affair, have somebody suddenly come in with a gun and threaten to shoot one of them, in order to reveal that the boy loves the girl. That is going too far.

Sometimes your plot device is too broad; sometimes too narrow. The *climactic situation* must always break in key with the quality of the story.

A lot of playwrights think it is a cute idea when writing a comedy to have it suddenly turn very dramatic at the end of the second act. I staged a play where that happened once. The author brought a tragic note into a light comedy at the end of the second act. The audience resented it. The curtain has a tremendous impact in a theater. I don't know of anything in any art that has a greater emphasis than the curtain in the theater. Your climactic situation at the end of your acts must always break in key with your story.

When you are writing your play, see your people in the process of living. Don't just have them come into a room and talk. That gives the poor director the job of having to think of what in the world he can do to make those people seem real and natural and human. Give them some employment yourself.

What to write about? I don't know. It is a very difficult thing to decide. Choice of material can be a happy accident, or an unfortunate selection. Knowledge of the theater develops an instinctive feeling towards material. Owen Davis said in his book, a play is a success or failure before the author starts to write it. That is something to give us all pause. Once in a while you hit upon an idea that is fresh, that is novel, that has some unusual quality in it.

Elmer Rice's *Street Scene* had such an idea. The minute he hit upon the idea of laying the scene of his play in front of a row of brownstone houses, he had something. The minute John Cecil Holm, who wrote *Three Men on a Horse*, thought of that character, that little fellow who wrote gift-card verses and who liked to place imaginary bets on horses, he had something. The freshness of a play can be found in its plot, characters, story, timeliness, threats to the audience's sympathies, any one or more of these elements. There has to be something fresh. You don't see many stories about—this sounds as though I am boasting, but the credit belongs to Clarence Day—about somebody desperately determined to get her husband baptized. Watch for that freshness.

A play doesn't have to point to a moral. You don't have to have a theme. Human nature is a good enough theme. You don't have to define God or tell what is wrong with the world, or anything like that. If you want to, that is fine, and I respect the dramatist who can do it. But it is enough for us to see human beings acting in the circumstances of life. That is rewarding if well done, without the play preaching a sermon.

If you are going to write what is called a propaganda play, don't let any character in the play know what the propaganda is. Act it out. Don't talk it out. Keep your characters from finding out what you are trying to prove. It will be exposed in your story, because it will be demonstrated in front of the audience. But the minute one of the characters finds out what points you are trying to make, that character will talk and talk and talk, and your play will become self-conscious.

This is another important thing. As soon as you have finished your play, don't send it right out to a producer or to an agent. I know from my own experience that when you have finished a scene and pulled it out of the typewriter, you say to yourself, "This thing is swell." You think it is about as good as you can possibly write. Let it cool for at least two months, and then go back and read it. Do your rewriting before the producer gets it. It is much easier all around.

I learned another thing from my first play, by Bert Robertson and myself, called *Tommy.* We opened in Atlantic City, and I thought it was a homely little comedy, you know; sort of the-first-year-of-school play-writing. We thought we had a whale of a finish to the second act; we thought it would be both a laugh and a tear, which is pretty valuable. Well, it was neither. It was about as bad a curtain as you can imagine. Simply dreadful. A very wise old producer put it on, George C. Tyler. We went back to the hotel with him, and he said, "You've got to get another end to the second act." We said, "No question about that, Mr. Tyler." He leaned back in his chair and began to think. Then he said, "What's the biggest laugh in the second act?" We finally came to the conclusion that it was such and such a line.

> TYLER: Get that line down to the curtain.
> WE: Well, look, that's the father's line.
> TYLER: Yeah, I know.
> WE: Well, he isn't on stage.
> TYLER: Get him on stage.
> WE: Look, Mr. Tyler, the line's not funny unless it's said in front of his wife.
> TYLER: Well, get her on stage!
> WE: Well, I don't know, I mean after all, Mr. Tyler, the way the story's . . .
> TYLER: Go upstairs and do it!

So we went upstairs and we did. We got the wife on, and we got the husband on, and we pulled this line. It won't seem like a very funny line to you, but in context it was a very big laugh. The father flares up and orders the boy out of the house. He says, "Why, that's the dirtiest trick that's been played on me since my marriage!" It doesn't sound funny, but it was. [Pause.] It was! He was a funny little fellow, and his wife took it personally! [Laughter.] Well, we got that laugh down to the curtain.

Now, to go on reminiscing if you want me to. My wife, Dorothy Stickney—she was my fiancée at the time—opened in a play shortly after this called *Chicago*. George Abbott staged it. I went down to Atlantic City to see it open. (My show was in Boston, waiting to come into New York.) There was a scene in *Chicago* where Francine Larrimore got a whale of a laugh and then there were two lines more and the curtain came down. So I got a hold of Abbott, whom I knew quite well, and I said, "Look, George"—I'd just learned this and was glad to show off, you know—I said, "George, in the scene with the lady interviewer, why don't you pull that line down to the curtain." He said, "Which line?" and I said, "You know, where the girl says to the sob sister, 'Why, I'm very refined. I was born in a convent.'" Abbott looked down at me from his height and said, "Do you think I'd ring down on a gag?"

I went out on the boardwalk and had a long talk with myself. Here was a man with ideals, by God! Here was a man who wouldn't cheapen himself that way. So I went back to New York, and I told my collaborator that this was unbecoming of us, and then I told Mr. Tyler that we shouldn't ring down on a gag and he said, "Well, why not?" We went ahead and rang down on the gag. And when *Chicago* came in to New York, you know, they rang down on the gag too!

PHOTOGRAPH BY ARNOLD NEWMAN.

Abe Burrows

(1910–1984)

At the piano sat a balding man who was invited to parties because he would gladly sing, in an absolutely terrible voice, such original compositions as "The Girl with the Three Blue Eyes—and What Makes Her Different" or "If You Were the Only Girl in the World and I Were the Only Boy—OK! But Right Now Leave Me Alone."

Abe Burrows was a funny man who couldn't write during the day because "the sun was shining." But he could write at night. For ten years, beginning in 1938, his work in radio was a major comic ingredient in *This Is New York, Texaco Star Theater, The Rudy Vallee Show, Duffy's Tavern, The Dinah Shore Show, The Abe Burrows Show,* and *Breakfast with Burrows.*

In 1951, at the invitation of Broadway producers Cy Feuer and Ernie Martin, he cowrote the Tony Award–winning musical *Guys and Dolls.* The composer and lyricist was Frank Loesser. The show was one of the greatest successes in Broadway history, running more than twelve hundred performances and becoming an enduring American classic. Burrows followed this with scripts for *Can-Can* (1953) and *Silk Stockings* (1955), both with words and music by Cole Porter; *Say, Darling* (1958); and *How to Succeed in Business Without Really Trying* (1961), which received the Pulitzer Prize and the Tony Award.

Double talented, he was now in double demand. As a director he staged *Two on the Aisle* (1952), *Can-Can* (1953), *Happy Hunting* (1956), *Golden Fleecing* (1959), *First Impressions* (1959), and *What Makes Sammy Run* (1964).

When George S. Kaufman was in rehearsal with *Silk Stockings* in Philadelphia, he did not feel able to cope with the necessary rewrites. He called Abe Burrows for help. Burrows came in to provide the expert doctoring needed to give *Silk Stockings* a profitable run. With this, Abe added a new career as one of the most sought after play doctors in the business.

Abram Burrows was born on December 18, 1910, in New York City. He graduated from Brooklyn's New Utrecht High School in 1928 and attended City College of New York and New York University. Burrows worked for an accounting firm and on Wall Street, first as a messenger and eventually as "a customers' man."

It was no secret that Burrows tended to be overweight and on one occasion was ordered to a "fat farm" by his doctor. This was severe medicine for Abe. He had been there for a week when his friend Cy Feuer phoned to ask how he was getting along. "Terrible!" moaned Abe. "They're starving me to death. I've got to get out of here." Feuer was all sympathy. "Would it help," he asked, "if I came up to visit you?" "Sure. But Cy, when you come, bring me a file with a cake in it."

PHOTOGRAPH BY PARRY STUDIO.

Russel McKinley Crouse
(1893–1966)

He was known to his friends and colleagues as "Buck." None were certain whether the nickname was derived from the nom de plume of a contemporary prizefighter or from his oft-demonstrated ability to enliven a party with a popular dance step, the buck-and-wing. All agreed that Russel Crouse was a pleasure to be with. His gentle and sunny disposition, his kindness, his wit—uncorroded by malice—were lifelong characteristics.

At seventeen, Russel Crouse went to work as a cub reporter for the *Cincinnati Commercial Tribune;* at eighteen, for the *Kansas City Star;* then for the *New York Globe,* the *Morning Mail,* and the *New York Post.* He ultimately became press agent for the Theater Guild.

Crouse's collaboration with Howard Lindsay began in 1934 with the successful musical *Anything Goes.* The original librettist had submitted an unsatisfactory piece of work and the desperate producer, Vinton Freedley, appealed to director Lindsay to take on the rewrite. Lindsay agreed on the condition that Freedley find him a collaborator.

How Freedley settled on Crouse is a mystery, but collaborate they did. *Anything Goes* was followed by *Red Hot and Blue* (1936), *Hooray for What* (1937), *Life with Father* (1939), *Strip for Action* (1942), the Pulitzer

Prize–winning *State of the Union* (1945), *Life with Mother* (1948), *Call Me Madam* (1950), *Remains to Be Seen* (1951), *The Prescott Proposals* (1953), *The Great Sebastians* (1956), *Happy Hunting* (1956), *Tall Story* (1959), *The Sound of Music* (1959), and *Mr. President* (1962). The two men also coproduced *Arsenic and Old Lace, The Hasty Heart, Detective Story, One Bright Day,* and *The Great Sebastians.* Prior to collaborating with Howard Lindsay, Crouse wrote the books for the musicals *The Gang's All Here* (1931) and *Hold Your Horses* (1933).

A New Dramatists Craft Discussion

with Abe Burrows
January 21, 1957

Howard Lindsay and Russel Crouse Are Cohosts.

MR. BURROWS: I noticed in the paper that I was to talk on "How to Write a Musical Comedy." That's a ridiculous premise. All I can say is how *not* to write a musical comedy, perhaps. And I think the first thing I'd like to start off with is, *why* write a musical comedy? Now, I know there're a lot of people running around who want to write a musical. One day I got a call from a guy who wanted to make a musical out of *South Pacific*. He said, "Put new tunes in, and we've got another show." [Laughter.]

I suspect the motive behind all this is to make a dollar. Musicals seem to be so successful; but at the risk of sounding wildly idealistic, that is a bum premise for a playwright. I've never known anyone in this business to set out to make money and make it. I don't know why.

The basic motive for doing a musical is that this story, this idea, can best be presented as a musical. The idea of doing a play plus tunes is a bad one. Because then you've got a play plus tunes and you haven't got a unity. Now, if you tell me that you think you've got an idea which music can help emotionally, where the underlying values of a story can be brought out emotionally by music, fine, that's one good reason for doing a musical. Another good reason is if you have someone like Ethel Merman, who not only sells tickets, bless her little heart, but if you want to realize Ethel's full value you must have music. It would be like telling the story of an oboe player without an oboe. There has to be an underlying reason for a musical.

I think it stems basically from what I think is the greatest of all art forms—opera. Opera combines all the reasons completely. Opera is absorbing because underlying all of it is music adding emotional value that a line of dialogue could never convey, a love scene couldn't convey. I've seen *La Bohème* thirty-five times, and it's always a new love story to me. Something happens under this love story that I know, that I've followed before, and then comes a strain of music that no line of dialogue could replace. That's the essence of the use of music. Whether it's musical comedy, light opera, operetta, or whatever. So you have to say, "Can music help?"

Now, the basic way most guys approach it today is they say, "I've got an idea for a wonderful musical." They have the "justified musical." You say, "Why do you want to do a musical?" And they say, "Well, I've got a great scene in a nightclub. You can get a great tune in there, you know. And then we got a scene in rehearsal—and more like that!" Well, that kind of justified thing gets very boring when it comes to sixteen tunes, which is about what a musical runs to. Another guy says, "Well, we've got a lot of songs here that are going to advance the plot."

That's another line. It's all right to have songs that advance the plot, but basically even if the song is kind of advancing the plot, I personally think a plot-wise action would advance the plot better than a song. All a song does is take longer. A song must be something in itself, either be tremendously entertaining, or be something you can't wait to hear again—and if it's up to the composer, you will hear it again. [Laughter.] Or it must have some emotional thing under it that gives you something, like Brunnhilde singing to her father in the third act of *Die Walküre.* You go to that opera, you don't know German, people don't act very much, they just stand there like stones. It's dark on the stage. [Laughter.] The girl's talking to her father as Harry Kurnitz once said, "He comes from a very good family—he's God!" [Laughter.]

An absurd situation—two hours in the Met. Boy, you think you're lost. Then comes this third act and she's talking to her father and there's the music and all of a sudden, you're crying. You're so moved you're shaking. That's the reason for using music. Either you're shaking, crying, or laughing, but you damn well better be doing something! That's why I always challenge a musical idea. I always ask, "Why are you doing it?"

Now comes the next thing. A fellow says, "I'm gonna do the book for a musical." Book is a libretto [laughter]—*libretto* means "little book." Actually, without the music and without the songs, it's a crippled book. Anybody who says, "I'm going to do a book for a musical and then I will get in touch with someone who will add songs," or does some of the lyrics, or, even worse than that, indicates, "Here they sing a song about how good it is to be in Paris,"—that infuriates every songwriter instantly. [Laughter.]

He doesn't know that a musical is a collaboration. It's the truest of all theater collaborations. In a musical, the librettists, the composers, the choreographer, if possible, are a team. In the case of *Oklahoma!,* the choreographer Agnes de Mille was a great creative factor.

Now, these all meet together. In other words, you can't think up an idea, for example, for a song without regard to the musical concept. You set up a scene on the balcony where the boy's carrying the girl around on a two-wheel bicycle and she's riding on his shoulders and the composer looks at you and says, "Just a minute, Abe, I've got a song just like that; I've saved your scene!" You see, he thinks with you, because in a musical what you can say musically is very important. And therefore these people must be with you. It must be a total collaboration at the beginning.

Mr. Lindsay: I want to specifically disagree with Abe when he leaves out the big element of working with the director.

Mr. Burrows: Well, that was just modesty on my part.

Mr. Crouse: But that's definitely part of the collaboration.

Mr. Burrows: Didn't someone once say—Hitler or somebody (joke)— that musicals aren't written, they're fixed? You sit down to write a musical and you're all bound up with the physical nature of a show. The mere fact that it'll take forty seconds to move something into place, or change something, will force you to do a new scene, something that will fill in. This is sort of separate from everything you've ever learned about playwriting. For instance, if I said, "Now this scene, Mr. Playwright, this scene of yours is fine but you've got to give me a small scene before it while the fellow sells popcorn," you would stare and look stunned.

But suppose the popcorn was essential there? Musicals are kind of like that. A guy says, "Gimme something here because Ethel needs three minutes to get into that damn gown." You say, "Well, wait a minute! Wear something quicker." No, you don't do it like that. You've got to work out something that'll take care of that delay.

Mr. Crouse: Now that's why I think that one of the boys we shouldn't have left out, although Howard mentioned him, is the scenic designer. Lots of times he can help you tremendously by getting from scene to scene without those delaying scenes you've been talking about. Without the crossovers which look false in a musical.

MR. BURROWS: If you can get him in at the beginning, it's good.

MR. CROUSE: I've seen several musicals that I think were ruined by playing scenes in sets that were much too deep in perspective and you lost the whole feeling of a scene because of it. I've seen lighting ruin comedy scenes because comedy has to be played in very bright light. Comedy is not only dependent on what people say, but on what they look like sometimes. The slight movement of the eyes can add to the laugh of a line. I think the designer coming in early can help tremendously, especially if he understands musicals. Including him in the early team is the best step to collaboration.

MR. BURROWS: You know, the physical nature of theater is a terribly important thing and too many playwrights, in their approach to theater, are too occupied with just the thought and the word. I think [Jo] Mielziner's concept of *Death of a Salesman* was an enormous help in the way that play finally came off.

In the theater, you think of the physical theater and the marvelous things we can do with it. We can't do the movies, the good things they do; but ours are better. You show a trick on the stage and people are delighted.

MR. LINDSAY: Mr. Crouse has already spoken of the scenes that need intimacy, comedy scenes and romantic scenes. But you get a chorus of thirty-two people, they can't dance in an intimate set, they've got to have full stage. So you see, all of these things have to be in your plan, in your original conception all the time. The very looseness, the varied elements begin to force things on you. There's a song; you've got to stop the story, though your story shouldn't really stop. But you arrive at a point where a song will capitalize a situation, and exploit it.

MR. BURROWS: Now we go into the difference between drama and story. A song can tell a story if you mean to emotionally convey what's going on in a way that a word couldn't. And you can do it in rhyme.

MR. LINDSAY: An odd thing is if it's a joke and it rhymes, it's funnier.

MR. BURROWS: I think one of the big weaknesses in the musical theater is the limitations of the composer. How many composers are there who can really tell emotionally what you're trying to push forward? Not very many. And they're not Wagner and they're not Puccini. They're guys who do their best, but they hit a ceiling, frequently, of a pop song.

MR. CROUSE: Of course they sometimes do that deliberately because the pop song is what sells copies and goes on the air. It can be of great help to your play.

MR. BURROWS: It's a funny thing, actually. I think the reason you fellows did the show with Ethel is the presentation of a musical person like that. You'd be out of your minds not to. It would be like doing a picture with Marilyn Monroe and not having a love scene.

MR. LINDSAY: Well, this was the fourth show we'd done with Merman. We're very fond of her, like to work with her; she's a great professional.

MR. BURROWS: Remember just one more basic thing, one ghastly thing about writing a musical. There's about an hour and ten minutes of dialogue in the average musical. That means you don't ever have time for a nice fat expository scene telling who the hero is and why he loves the girl, and what the girl's character is and where she came from and what her father did. You have to have the fast, broad stroke.

When I'm directing something, I try to help in that department by casting, even typecasting. When a girl walks on the stage, I like to know why the guy's stuck on her. Right away without explaining it. Typecasting. Let's take the value judgment out of that phrase because it creates a terrible shudder all over the Actors Studio. [Laughter.]

When I say typecasting, I mean get people who come pretty close to what you have in mind in your play and don't hope that an actor who's intelligent enough, given six months to find the character, might get it in time for you to close in New York. But the scenes must be shorter, sharper, the point must be made quicker; it's all got to jell fast, happen quickly, be of such basic substance that the intrusion of a three- or four-minute number won't make you forget the plot.

MR. LINDSAY: I think we ought to say something about the market, since we're professionals and have to earn our living as writers. There just isn't any market for a written book. That's not the way musicals are done.

MR. BURROWS: There is this possibility: Two people, a composer and a librettist, get together. They say, "This would make a musical." Then they try to sound out a director, a producer, or a star.

MR. LINDSAY: Usually you have to capture your star or producer with the idea—it's the idea that has to be attractive to somebody. And I think it's more often done on an idea than on a full, written book.

MR. CROUSE: That was true of *Call Me Madam*. The idea sold Merman and sold Berlin.

MR. LINDSAY: Yes, the idea that Merman would play an ambassador abroad.

MR. BURROWS: With, I recall, one song, Howard.

QUESTION: What about the conventions of a musical?

MR. BURROWS: In the musical you have the fast leap and everyone rushes for their hats, that's convention. [Laughter.] It's called the hat number. I remember in *Guys and Dolls*, there were the people in terrible trouble. The boy had left for Las Vegas, the gambler, Nathan Detroit, and he was never going to look at this girl and "never get foot on her again," as he put it, and what happens? The next scene they're getting married and everyone's delighted. That's the fast leap. Like the short stories end in the *New Yorker:* "He stood there regarding the stump of his bleeding arm." [Laughter.]

MR. LINDSAY: That's a great musical idea! [Laughter.]

MR. CROUSE: I remember a musical, Abe, with Ed Wynn when he looked at his watch and said, "It's ten minutes after eleven. You ought to marry her, and you ought to marry him," and we brought the curtain down! [Laughter.]

MR. BURROWS: Well, this sounds like a quick ending but it really is craftsmanship because they've been in that theater two and a half hours. You've made your point and if you attempt with music to really resolve the inner depths, you're going to have the Ring Cycle, and that takes four weeks. I do think you can have quality if you think in terms of the short thing. You get a quality in the fast vignette and the fast sketch.

Certain playwrights who've tried to do musicals have floundered, because they suffered from not having an opportunity to develop in depth, when it should have been left to the composer. When the guy in *South Pacific* starts to sing "Some Enchanted Evening," you know as much about those people as you ever care to know. That's exploration and depth truly. But that's Dick Rodgers. And there are very few of him around. [Laughter.]

QUESTION: Mr. Burrows, is there a justification for saying that there are certain conventions in the musical theater that are laid out ahead of time, that you don't have to worry about such a thing as motivation? In a musical play the boy and the girl walk on stage, you know he's the boy and she's the girl and you don't [laughter] have to say they're going to be lovers.

MR. BURROWS: The whole theater is a convention. You know darn well those people are up on a stage. There's a proscenium arch, which is the basic convention of all. The acceptance of proscenium arch, footlights, program rattling, that's all convention. You accept it. But I think if you go too much for accepting convention, you may end up with bad theater. I mean, you've got to put a surprise in there. Though I remember when I was writing *Guys and Dolls*, breaking my skull trying to put suspense into whether the girl would go to Havana with the guy, George Kaufman saying to me, he was the director, "Now look, Abe, it already says!" [Bangs on table.] [Laughter.]

But just as there is convention in the theater, so the audience will accept suspense and tensions and pressures on your level. At the end of the first-act curtain, when you separate your lovers, which you have to do [laughter]—actually, your first-act curtain is the same as your second-act curtain in a three-act play—you're trying to create anxiety. You've got to make the audience worry. Now, they don't really worry. They know—kinda—that Ethel Merman and Fernando Lamas are going to get back together. If you do it for them well, they'll buy your premise and worry.

MR. LINDSAY: They're worrying over *how* at least.

MR. BURROWS: If you're a writer and they're trusting you, they'll accept your basic concept. If I were standing up and telling you a long joke, but

I was telling it interestingly, you'd listen. You know it's gonna be a joke, I'm going to fool you. Then I pull the twist, and you laugh or cry, as the case may be.

There are guys who rely too much on conventions. You know Hollywood. They always used to make that joke: "Why does this girl fall in love? What's the motivation!" The motivation that Irving Thalberg once gave is, "He's Clark Gable!" [Laughter.] That is basic truth typecasting. You put a guy on stage and you see immediately—in a surface fashion—why a woman is attracted to him. But after that, his actions must be such that she continues to be attracted to him. He can't behave like a heel or he'll lose her and the audience. It's an odd thing in writing for the theater—to learn to tread that fine line between accepting conventions and not relying on them.

QUESTION: I want to get back to your statement of the musical as a sort of integration of the arts. I'm wondering if this applies in toto to the musical adaptations on the stage today, since most of them start out as adaptations of already successful art forms, the novel, the play.

MR. BURROWS: I never look on the adaptation in that way. I know that it's become a cliché thing to say that Shakespeare was almost completely an adapter, using stories from old Italian legends or something else. In a sense when a man writes *Henry V* he's adapting history.

In *Guys and Dolls,* I took a Runyon short story and built on a superstructure of a larger story. I used a little legend that Damon had about a gambler who fell in love with a mission doll and finally converted. That was about the whole story. And that was based on a true story about a girl named Reba Crawford who was a Follies girl and became an evangelist. Damon adapted that and I adapted from him, both building superstructure. Look at Bizet. *Carmen* is an adaptation from Mérimée's novel and makes a whole new art form.

I was commenting on the perfectly integrated opera. The musicals can't attain it for what I think is a very tough reason. We've got a great many pretty good artists writing musical librettos. I think you have the best choreographers in the world doing choreography for them. But the composers—outside of a few—haven't got the artistic stature. Their music is tuneful, but it fails to move you emotionally. That's where they fail.

QUESTION: Have you found there are certain kinds of materials, certain kinds of situations that you can say, "Well, this should be a musical because of the material or it should be a play because of the type"?

MR. BURROWS: Yes, frequently. It's a hard thing to judge. But sometimes you may have something where you say, "Oh boy, this kind of fellow and this kind of girl, would I love it if instead of this kind of inhibited love scene I have here—if they could sing at each other." And that may be valid. You say, "If only I could get a composer who could say these things."

In *La Bohème* they say all sorts of things, like my name is Mimi but it's really Lucia and I sell flowers. But underneath it Puccini is playing stuff—[laughter] and it's a great, great love scene. He says, "Your tiny hand is frozen. Your hand is cold." And she says, "Sure my hand is cold. It's cold here." But the guy sings it and the whole place comes apart. [Laughter.] The music says something that the author was incapable of. Puccini always chose hacks anyway.

MR. LINDSAY: That was pretty good material.

MR. BURROWS: Oh, the story's a good story. But it needed the music plus a story where the play itself didn't tell it because it's a rather loosely constructed play and the music holds it together.

MR. CROUSE: Generally you need one bright guy to guide it and even hold auditions to raise money for production. I remember Herman Levin had one, I think it was for *Gentlemen Prefer Blondes*. They had forty-five well-selected people with a lot of money. He told me later that "not only did I not raise a dime, but I had my best umbrella stolen." [Laughter.]

QUESTION: Mr. Burrows, I was production observer on *Make a Wish*.

MR. BURROWS: Gee, that was a dog. That was one I doctored.

QUESTION: I'd like to know something about the doctoring because it would not only tell us about musical comedy but about playwriting.

MR. BURROWS: I've been accused of doctoring a lot more shows than I have. Every time I go out of town, people think I'm there to fix something, even if it's own show. But *Make a Wish* came right after *Guys and Dolls* and I was well thought of at the moment and there was this disastrous thing happening in Philly. The original author, Preston

Sturges, had abandoned the show so they had no author in Philadelphia. A friend of mine was involved in the production and he had had some very important people in as backers and he said, "Abe, could you help us? I know you can't pull this thing out, but would you see to it that no one gets hit with picks?"

I went down there with some friends of mine and felt a great deal of pity for this huge, glittering turkey dying on the stage. [Laughter.] Very sad. There's something about a show—it takes on a life of its own. And suddenly you don't care as much about the other people involved as the people on that stage gasping for breath and trying to do something. I did a little work and it wasn't a disaster, but I could never fix the basic fault. When you're doctoring a show, everyone's sick and miserable and low and feeling awful. You arrive fresh, well fed; you've had dinner on the train, a couple of drinks; you're not in trouble—they are. You've got a hit show running and they're gasping in Philadelphia. It's like a doctor. You're sick and the doctor arrives and he's kind of clean looking and you're . . . [Laughter.]

You do it quickly. You redirect it, you change the pace, and also, your presence generally increases cast morale. Because by this time, they hate the director, no one's speaking to anyone. But you lift the morale in general and all of a sudden everybody gets happy. Then I really worked them hard. These people needed not only pace, but they needed to be tired out a bit. I had a dress rehearsal that morning—the morning of opening night! And then on opening night, I said, "If anyone stops to breathe for one second, I'll shoot him from the box!" And boy, it went by and was fast and tuneful. [Laughter.]

But in *Make a Wish*, I could put in a few pleasant things. I remember we got six good notices and one pan. But it didn't run. It had an incurable sickness. It was a bad idea in the first place.

MR. LINDSAY: You said no one was speaking to the director. When a show out of town is in trouble, they always pick out someone not to speak to. It can be the producer, the director, or the author, and as a last resort, the press agent.

MR. BURROWS: But when a director loses, you're dead. I've seen authors not speaking to directors, actors not speaking to authors, but when the actors don't talk to the director, then you're in terrible trouble.

QUESTION: You were talking about somebody pulling the show together and getting the director in early. You may not want to talk about it, but do you know the history of *Candide*? Why didn't it pull together? [Laughter.]

MR. BURROWS: That's a good example of what we were talking about. I think what happened there—the sickness there—was that the idea of making a musical out of *Candide* could only have been thought of some moment in the moonlight on the deck of a ship that was under water. [Laughter.] Lennie Bernstein is a very talented, very wonderful guy; Lillian Hellman's very bright. I think their enthusiasm swept old Tyrone Guthrie up, and I think they never came down to earth until they were in trouble in Boston. It should never have been put on. They never knew what it was.

Someone said, "Wouldn't *Candide* make a wonderful musical?" [Laughter.] That was like Julius Caesar saying on the fifteenth of March, "I think I'll take a walk in the forum." [Laughter.]

QUESTION: *Pygmalion* at one time seemed most unlikely . . .

MR. BURROWS: It would seem difficult to do, but with *My Fair Lady* they saw a way. Forgetting the fact that it's the biggest hit of all time—I think it's wonderful. But the great thing about it is, they didn't adapt the play. They adapted the movie. Now the movie of *Pygmalion* was Pascal's [the movie's producer] conception of adding romance to a play that has none at all. I doubt if *My Fair Lady* could ever have been written had the movie *Pygmalion* never been done. In the credits, they credit it to the movie.

Shaw had an epilogue to *Pygmalion* in which he told why Liza could not marry Henry Higgins and never would and would probably wind up with the other fellow. Then came the movie, which added romance, and you felt that Leslie Howard was in love with Wendy Hiller, basically because of typecasting. From there they got the romantic aspect of *My Fair Lady*. And, of course, what they did to decorate it. I've always felt that Alan Lerner, in that one, should be given credit not only for what he did, but for what he didn't do. The enormous pace, the wonderful things! What he added was always in the level—and I loved that. But it is an adaptation of the movie and if you're a man who never saw the movie and just read the play and you loved it—*My Fair Lady* might annoy you very much.

QUESTION: Who did the movie script?

MR. BURROWS: Shaw and Pascal.

QUESTION: "The Rain in Spain" isn't in the play. It's only in the movie.

MR. BURROWS: As a matter of fact, almost none of that scene is in the play. That is a case by the way—we were talking about musical excitement—that is a perfect example. Fritz Loewe and Alan Lerner took "The rain in Spain lies mainly in the plain," and when she finally gets the enunciation right, with the music, they did something they'd probably never get with dialogue. They lifted you with such joy! You might write a scene and she says, "The rain in Spain lies mainly in the plain," and he says, "Very good, Liza."

MR. CROUSE: But they built this up to a musical crescendo . . .

MR. BURROWS: And the guy could dance. That was a wonderful, musical use of it. They even took some of the songs out of Shaw's prologue. "Why can't the English teach their children how to speak?" is in Shaw's prologue to *Pygmalion*. The opening notes! That very line!

QUESTION: There was a writer in the *New York Times* who felt this is a period of hit-going rather than play-going. If a play isn't a hit, it has no chance for survival. Do you agree with that?

MR. BURROWS: Yes, unfortunately. There are several reasons for going to the theater. Some people go to exchange views with the author, which, I think, is the basic reason for going. If the play's about people you don't like to go to dinner with, you want to see why. And if it's about people you don't like to go to dinner with but the people are written by Strindberg, I like to see it. So, you go to exchange views.

But the mass of people in New York and London go for illusion. They go to be taken out of their world. Maybe they can secretly be given an insight—but basically they go to be taken out of themselves for a moment. They go to identify with a character up there on the stage, for catharsis, or whatever reason.

QUESTION: Well, what I had in mind is that a playwright sitting down to write a play has a particular hit idea in the back of his mind. In other words, if it's not a terrific hit, he's nowhere.

MR. LINDSAY: If he writes with the idea of its being a hit, then he's wrong. He must write it to be a success, but if he writes it for that big money . . .

MR. BURROWS: As Howard says, you can't write to make a thing a hit. You've got to write what you're thinking of, what you want to say. I personally think that whatever the subject and whoever the people are you're writing about, if you tell it well and with integrity and stick to it, I think someone's gonna want to hear it. If you've got something to say. I think one of the best plays I've seen in my lifetime is *Waiting for Godot*. I think it'll eventually become part of the American scene. *Threepenny Opera* was a tremendous flop in 1935. Now it's gonna run forever.

QUESTION: The other day I was talking to two foreign actors about a play, Maxim Gorky's *Living Corpse*, and talking about Gorky being a very tender, sensitive person. Now, this springs from his people's culture. They're unafraid to be tender. And to cry. But, can you do that for an American audience? I look around me and men don't cry.

MR. BURROWS: Sure, but the point is, there is a way to reach them. In other words, I think it's a problem of communication. I think the American people, culturally now, in many ways are in a bad way as far as love and tenderness is concerned. Take a look at our divorce rate and what goes on in mental hospitals. We've got a pretty tense society. There must be a way to talk to it.

There are people who can reach psychotics. Why can't we reach a disturbed public? If the playwright is a man who feels no tenderness—I don't say he has to know it; it might be sublimated—but if he hasn't got it someway, he can't put it out. But if he puts it out and does it well, people will buy it. They'll cry. I've cried in the theater a few times.

QUESTION: You said a little while ago that musicals usually have romance and illusion in them, and that one reason they're so successful is that people get it here where they don't get it in straight plays. A little later, it was indicated that people didn't seem to want that in straight plays. Well, there seems to be some kind of contradiction.

Mr. Burrows: Yeah, but in a musical they're getting it kinda by injection, the unconscious effect of emotional music. I think they want it but they won't admit it, while in a musical they accept it.

Question: With *Guys and Dolls*, did you ever think of making it a straight play?

Mr. Burrows: No. It was sort of a cartoon in a sense. It had people who weren't real people; all of them were kind of off the ground. It turns out the Runyon stuff was continually unsuccessful in straight plays.

Mr. Lindsay: You're right. His characters were supposed to be such wonderful Broadway types, but they never existed.

Mr. Burrows: No, they were all cartoons, that's why a musical thing had to float them. I think that's why it worked.

Mr. Crouse: It was difficult to make them living people.

Mr. Burrows: Actually, in *Guys and Dolls* the most successful couple were two people who weren't in Runyon's book, Nathan and Adelaide. Nathan was just mentioned by name. But there the romance was a kind of true one. You never really believed the romance between the mission doll and the gambler. That was really a phony romance. But they believed the other one.

Question: You three gentlemen have a great reputation for humor and I wonder if something could be said about what you think the essence of humor is; or at least, how one should approach the writing of something which is humorous in its whole point of view.

Mr. Lindsay: Well, the only explanation I've ever heard was given by a friend of mine years ago. He used it first about an actor who fooled him. My friend had written a sketch for the Lambs, and he was staging it and he cast this actor he was very sure of and someone said, "How's it going?" And my friend said, "So and so's going to be terrible," and the other said, "He is?" and my friend said, "Yes, because he can't think funny." And that is the only phrase I know that really describes comedy. The comedian thinks funny. The writer of comedy thinks funny. Humor is an instinct.

MR. BURROWS: I think humor's darn close to being congenital. It's a way of talking, just as some kids walk with their toes turned in. Every child as he grows up develops a kind of adjustment to life. Some kids cry, some kids wall themselves in, some kids learn to fight back and argue. Other kids learn that they can use a joke to adjust themselves to their problem.

The joke was always my method of getting out of or into trouble. My father was that way. Humor is just a way of writing. And some people can do it and some can't. A profound insight. Shaw could snap a joke every time he needed one. Wilde could. Ibsen had real trouble. [Laughter.] Ibsen insisted to his dying day that *Enemy of the People* was comedy.

QUESTION: I always thought that comedy was used in its broad sense—like the human comedy, a comedy on life. For instance, *The Sea Gull* by Chekhov. You think, "Now this isn't very funny." But if you look at it in the broad, objective sense, you get the impression it's a comedy on human nature.

MR. BURROWS: Originally, it was the opposite of tragedy. Tragedy sprang from the religious ritual where they'd sacrifice a goat. That was the serious aspect.

MR. CROUSE: If the goat got away, it was a comedy. [Laughter.]

MR. BURROWS: If the goat got away! [Laughter.] And that's what I mean by jokes!

QUESTION: People used to do those things in theater, but now everybody's so bloody serious.

MR. LINDSAY: You mean the farce?

MR. BURROWS: You know, I've been arguing about that, and I think I know what happened to those kind of writers. They're in television. [Laughter.] The growth of radio and television siphoned them off. A friend of mine said to me recently, "So and so wants me to collaborate on a farce. I think we could make it a funny one. Do you think I should devote the time to it?"

MR. LINDSAY: Well, farce, in the form it used to be, is dead now. That's when the audience and writer agree in the first five minutes that nobody will believe anything that is going to happen, but if you play along it will be funny.

MR. BURROWS: Most people today, if you ask them the definition of a farce, will define it as something that's crazy, made up, and unbelievable, whereas I think the crux of a farce is believability.

If I define a farce, I think it's where the author contrives a premise and says to the audience, "Here is my premise. Will you buy it?" The audience then says, "Okay, your premise is that if this man has not paid the rent by two o'clock this afternoon his body will be sold to science." [Laughter.] As a matter of fact, I like that! [Laughter.] I must stay believable within my premise. They'll still buy a farce today, I think, if the premise is constructed in a way that the audience accepts it as bedrock.

QUESTION: Wasn't farce usually based on the contrived situation?

MR. BURROWS: With the preoccupation with character, there's no big rush for situation in the theater. You see, farce was the ultimate of stuff. Actually, that's what the word "farce" means in French—stuff. It was the ultimate of the made up, contrived situation. I think the dropping of farce came with the dropping of situation. The whole preoccupation has been with character and there's been a kind of abandonment of situation.

MR. LINDSAY: A friend of mine was talking to me about farce. He said, "You know, a farce doesn't have to have funny lines." At first I didn't get it. Then suddenly, I did. It's what happens that's funny.

MR. CROUSE: You get people into a funny situation, and no matter what happens, it's funny.

MR. BURROWS: I do think the guys who thought in contrived lines are today in TV and radio.

QUESTION: Today there seems to be a trend—straight farce and straight tragedy don't work, but put them together and you get a tragic farce.

MR. LINDSAY: Tragic farce? Such as? Can you give us an example?

MR. BURROWS: Well, what about *Arsenic and Old Lace*? A great tragic farce.

MR. LINDSAY: I wouldn't call it tragedy.

MR. CROUSE: More comedy-drama.

MR. BURROWS: Well, a lot of people got killed.

QUESTION: Chekhov is an example.

MR. BURROWS: *The Sea Gull* has terrific comedy mixed with tragic elements. Well, I think we all sound pretty confused now. [Laughter.]

PHOTOGRAPH BY INGE MORATH.

Arthur Miller

(1915–)

The title, conventional wisdom has it, occupies a crucial role in the commercial life of a play. So Arthur Miller was told, over and over again, by a number of concerned parties when *Death of a Salesman* was being put into production. "Death" in the title meant death at the box office. If it couldn't be drenched in sunshine, a title should at least sound a positive note.

The pressure for change was unremitting until one morning in Philadelphia, where *Salesman* was playing prior to coming to Broadway, the playwright walked into rehearsal with some news. The night before, a show had opened on the Great White Way and the critics had slaughtered it. The offering was called *Joy to the World*. Miller tossed the reviews on the table and said, "So much for happy titles." There was no more talk about changing the name of his play after that.

Born in New York City in 1915, Miller enjoyed a comfortable life until 1929, when the stock market collapse seriously affected his family economically. He worked at an auto-parts warehouse to earn the money for college and in his spare time read voluminously. Reading, he said, imbued him with the belief that writing can be a way of making sense out of apparent senselessness. At the University of Michigan in the

1930s, he turned to playwriting and won the university's Avery Hopwood Award two years running.

Miller's first play on Broadway, *The Man Who Had All the Luck* (1944), lasted, as he said, "four sad performances." But by 1956 he had written four plays that were both intellectually challenging and theatrically innovative: *All My Sons* (1947), *Death of a Salesman* (1949), *The Crucible* (1953), and *A View from the Bridge* (1955).

With the royalties from *All My Sons*, Miller bought a farm in Connecticut and built a studio with the express purpose of working on the play that possessed him—*Death of a Salesman*. His drama *The Crucible* began life as an allegory, drawing the parallel between the Communist witch-hunts of the '50s and the real witch-hunts of seventeenth-century Salem. Miller also wrote *After the Fall* (1964), *Incident at Vichy* (1964), and *The Price* (1969).

For his then-wife, the actress Marilyn Monroe, he wrote the movie *The Misfits*, which costarred Clark Gable (1961).

Among Miller's many accolades are Tony Awards for *All My Sons, Death of a Salesman,* and *The Crucible;* a Pulitzer Prize for *Salesman;* an Emmy for a TV version of *Salesman* (1967); and the John F. Kennedy Award for Lifetime Achievement (1984).

His autobiography, *Timebends: A Life*, was published in 1987.

With new plays, including *The Ride Down Mt. Morgan*, which was produced on Broadway in 2000, and regular revivals and productions throughout the world, Arthur Miller continues to be a dynamic force in the theater.

A New Dramatists Craft Discussion

with Arthur Miller
February 27, 1956

Mr. Miller is introduced by New Dramatist Ted Mabley.

MR. MABLEY: If I may start it off, I'd be very curious to hear about the idea of the little man today as the tragic hero. If I can paraphrase what you have said—that the little man's attempt to find his own place in the scheme of things—to assert his own dignity—would raise him to the level of a tragic hero. Am I correct?

MR. MILLER: It is true I have said certain things about this problem. The whole business came up in 1949–50 after *Death of a Salesman* because there seemed to be about the play a tragic feeling or mood. Yet some people thought that the play was impossible as a tragedy because the hero had none of the normal attributes of classic tragic heroes, primarily his social rank and nobility of mind, etcetera. I wanted to point out that these were not necessarily the exclusive qualities and that what was really involved was perhaps a thrust on the part of the play as a whole, and on the part of the character, toward an ultimate kind of reckoning for himself. When that thrust was made, that was the important thing—and the rank, etcetera, of the hero was of less importance. I ended up—quite rightly, I thought— defending what is called the common man as a possible tragic hero.

But as time has gone on I've made demands upon the hero for other reasons. I needed a greater ability on the part of the hero for self-realization, for self-consciousness. This is because I have changed and not because I have been trying to work with a definition of any kind. In other words, I still believe what I said is true, but I do think now that the essential element is the thrust towards weighing himself in the ultimate scales of life. The tragic hero is basically a fanatic. He cannot let himself go once he begins a course of action. He is an obsessed person. For example, the difference between Hamlet and Horatio: Hamlet says to Horatio, "I wish I could achieve a balance as you do. You're a sensitive man. You see what I see, but you're able to stop short of disasters, the path I seem to have to follow."

I think, given that kind of obsession with an ultimate value, with the ultimate desire to weigh himself on the ultimate scales, that is the essential thing. What I'm trying to get at now and have been through various means in *The Crucible* and *A View from the Bridge* is to achieve a kind of consciousness on the part of the character which is barred to Willy Loman. To achieve that, a new dimension has to be set into the play, the dimension of objectivity. In *A View from the Bridge*, one of the means of creating that consciousness was through the Narrator and the whole construction of the play; that's only one means. There can be others because the character depicted in the play is a man who can achieve for himself only an extremely small measure of self-awareness. The audience is left again with the job of creating conscious realization of what is happening. That is less true in tragic drama than in any succeeding drama. There is always a point in the Greek or Elizabethan play where somebody on the stage states in so many words what has been learned. Not in terms of an aphorism or a maxim, but in terms of an experiential statement of some sort, because they did believe in the ability of people to learn from their actions. This is something we grudgingly give to a dramatic character in our theater, in the whole realistic theater.

I'm trying to achieve that not for classic purposes, but because I believe that people do learn. They may not be able to apply what they learn. They may be helpless before the facts of their fate, but I think they do learn more than we give them credit for on the stage. I'm trying now to find a way to dramatize that naturally. We have a surprisingly low level of intelligence among the characters of our serious plays. It's no accident. It's not that playwrights are any more stupid than anybody else, but that there seems to be an unwillingness in our whole culture—not only in plays but also in fiction—to accept that objective ideas are derived by people in great emotional situations and that we are, as a result, writing visceral works. That is all right, some of them excellent, but there is something more.

I think the best example of the other reality is Shaw. We don't have to imitate. But I do think that we're losing and sacrificing a good deal in the realistic theater when we have no formal means of truthfully saying that people do gather from their experience. I don't think that life is quite as unintelligent as it often seems to be on the stage and I'm trying from my point of view to bring that dimension into the theater.

<u>MR. MABLEY</u>: Isn't it true that the audience had to supply that for Willy in *Death of a Salesman*?

<u>MR. MILLER</u>: Yes, they did. There are other characters, for instance, for whom that would not be quite good enough: people who have a higher degree of objectivity. Let us say you wrote about a scientist or a professor or some other intelligent, educated man whose tendency is to try to derive from his experience some pattern of knowledge so he can avoid his mistakes—so that he can discover and develop some philosophical outlook for his life. That's a legitimate character and I don't believe we have a play in the American repertory that has such a character at its heart. It's as though there were some distrust on the part of the people toward any character who can say on stage, "I see now that what I did was so and so . . ."

I think some stirring stuff could come out of a person of that sort. We deal with him in a more superficial kind of play sometimes. There's always a comedy about the college professor or the fantasy about people of intelligence, but there's never a tragic play about them; or else they are made effete. All this relates to whether the common man is the hero.

<u>QUESTION</u>: You're saying there is a growth from the inarticulate hero to the articulate hero. I wonder if, in this growth, there is also a growth of language?

<u>MR. MILLER</u>: As far as language is concerned, you have a cleavage between two sorts of plays, a play in verse and a play in prose. Verse is verse. You can fool with it just so far, but the form of verse is quite strict, recognizable, and there. The form of prose is much more malleable.

As long as the basic pretense of a play is to present life "as it is" and to make the audience forget it is in a theater by giving them an essentially subjective experience, so that they can forget who's sitting next to them, so that they identify themselves with the characters, and all of their empathic responses are flowing (which usually happens with us in a prose play), then you are within a certain form. The only way to get out of that form is the verse play.

We have plays in fine writing in the old academic sense. It is prose. It's often poetic prose, but it is realism. It is trying to heighten realism. The only different form is the verse form. To write that, one has to be a poet.

One has to be completely at home in the verse form. We have never had such a writer in this country.

The next best thing—I'm not speaking in terms of values now, but in terms of the proximity of one form to another—is the highly poeticized play, a play which is so concise, so symbolized, that it arrives at a species of poetry by virtue of the nature of the action rather than profoundly as a result of the words. Whether a real leap to verse form will take place is, I think, less a question of the pressure of cultural events on the theater than on literally the accidental rise in this theater of a true poet. There can be more or less a poetic diction in a prose play, but it will not materially alter the attack of the play on its material. The attack will always remain subjective, to make people feel they're not in the theater.

As soon as you create a verse play something else happens. An objectivity creeps into the play. We know that people are not speaking the way we do. There is, then, an attempt to enlarge the dimension of the theater (if the man is a great poet) by saying in effect to the audience, "You are in a theater. This was written by a writer. These people have not stumbled on these words by accident. They've learned them."

In other words, it becomes an art form, a self-conscious art form, which any verse play really is. That is the leap. If we get a poet, we'll have it. If we don't, we'll have more and more poetic, poeticized drama. Now that raises a lot of other problems as to what is really poetic drama and what is a spurious kind of escape from reality.

QUESTION: Are you saying that poetic drama is not subjective; would not have empathic responses from the audience—that you would not be able to identify with the character as much as in prose?

MR. MILLER: Each form has its virtues and its price. The grand virtue of the realistic theater is to create an atmosphere which is homey and effortless for the audience to identify with. You know the people are speaking as they do speak. The surroundings are utterly familiar, etcetera. The thing that is most difficult for the prose theater is to create meaning, symbolic meaning for the play, because it is essentially inarticulate.

The virtue of the verse drama is that it is not being spoken as things are spoken in real life. License is given to speak of those things which are on the playwright's mind but which, more specifically, are the meanings of the actions themselves. The playwright can, through this artifice, comment upon his scenes because that is the license given to him by common consent to his formalization of language. What is difficult to do in a verse play is to create empathy, familiarity, identification with the characters, for the simple reason that you have created an artifice between the audience and the stage which makes it very difficult for that identification to take place.

The number of prose written characters who are comprehensible and identifiable to the audience in our day are many times greater than the characters created in verse drama. I'm not speaking about poetic drama, but verse drama. There is an artifice standing between the audience and the stage which does, I think, obstruct an empathic response in our time. But a virtue of the verse is to hold the audience at a certain distance so that they are consciously aware of what is taking place, not only unconsciously being worked on.

Verse is a design and the wonderful part of it is that the audience can be aware of the design. As a matter of fact, the better the prose play, the more difficult it is to make an impact with design. The audience gets so wound up in the petty details of the action that when you say, "What does this play mean?" they say, "Mean?" The architecture of the play is more apparent when the play is more self-conscious. The verse obviously is there not only because of its beauty, but because it is possible through verse for the playwright to elucidate his meaning verbally.

QUESTION: Along the same line: A good young actor who is cast in an Elizabethan play immediately tries to see how he can make this part empathetic to the audience. He tries to make a prose drama out of the poetry.

MR. MILLER: That's a mistake. Given the design of a Shakespearean play you can't destroy that design, as many American actors unconsciously do, by speaking the language as if they had just happened to walk in the theater tonight. The design of a Shakespearean play is primarily its language. The scenes are written so that the language can flow. As soon as he gets to a place where the passion is less, there are prose passages and he gets away from them as fast as he can.

The actor should be able to encompass that verse—that is, to keep the design—fill it with passions that underlie it but never to violate it, try to pretend it isn't there. That won't work. He'll be stumbling over it all the time. He's got to admit it's there, but try to fill it with its underlying meaning.

QUESTION: Doesn't he still try to use it within the design?

MR. MILLER: Oh, I don't say that empathy is impossible in a verse play. I just say that its primary virtue is not that. It's obvious it isn't that, because our experience of life is a prose existence and we respond to the familiar much more rapidly than we do to the unfamiliar. As a playwright, if the object is to create a design, well it ought to be that—if that is the primary object.

We have a modern playwright, Bertolt Brecht, who is very involved with these problems, and he is a poet. His attempt is also to try to create a kind of objective theater. He's trying to do it without verse—without the Elizabethan forms; to create actions on the stage which will not involve the audience so profoundly emotionally in these actions that they will forget what they mean. Now, since he's living in a Communist society and is himself very Left, the excuse for this is that he wants to teach in the theater.

The Elizabethans had the same ideology, except that they were not trying to teach Marxism. To them, to put on an action that had no more-or-less clear design of meaning—well, it's obvious from the plays that they weren't interested in that. The lesser playwrights were very moralistic. They had epilogues which say if you do the following you're going to end up this way. There was a great attempt at objectifying the action by both Brecht and the Elizabethans. But he's doing it not so much through language as through theatrical designs of other kinds—anything to destroy the rapport of the audience that is so deadly to meaning.

Brecht says, "I'm not interested in titillating this audience—make them cry, laugh, or be moved, etcetera, for its own sake." He says, "I'm not a clown. I'm not an actor. I'm not a lesser artist than a writer—and as a writer I'm primarily a philosopher. As a philosopher, I want to create an architecture of meaning." So every time a play threatens to get too subjective, he breaks up the subjectivity. It's the difference between, let's say, Mozart and Rachmaninoff—a great outpouring of feeling as opposed to great feeling, but feeling that is strongly encased in the design.

QUESTION: A couple of years back, at the Circle in the Square, you said you had certain things that gave you trouble about the rather sentimental response to *Death of a Salesman.* You were talking about the possibility of critical distance between the audience and the play, as Brecht does with his things. In *A View from the Bridge*, the same thing applies to a degree when the Narrator creates an actual critical response during the action per se. Do you still feel that this is the direction that serious drama can go to achieve its greatest effect?

MR. MILLER: It is always heading in that direction. It is interesting to note that as a playwright gets older, he gets less and less patient with the machinery of emotion because you discover after a while that you can do that. You can make people weep. It's surprisingly easy. You can even make them laugh. Then after a while, due to developments in one's own life, it isn't enough. You begin casting about for ways of extracting from the subjective situation its thematic meaning.

Realism has a method of doing that. By joining one realistic detail to another we arrive at a tapestry. That tapestry has a design, and the audience is moved emotionally and arrives, through the experiencing of this emotion, at a concept. That is a perfectly valid form and I have nothing against it. It's just that when you do it enough, you can't get fired up to do it again.

The methods used to objectify the play are many. There is expressionism, there are all kinds of stylization, as well as verse drama, etcetera. What I'm driving at now is to create a drama that is subjective and only as real as the life of cognition. I am no longer interested in the play that opens with some distorted set and soft pastel lighting and garrulous characters.

QUESTION: But you're still dealing with an audience whose whole cultural pattern and stimuli are subjective twenty-four hours a day, whose thinking is toward a kind of nonobjectivity. Doesn't that make the writer who wants to write an objective play have an awfully difficult task?

MR. MILLER: It's against the grain of the whole culture. You see the end of it in television dramas. It goes towards the senselessly repeated "emotional" situations. It's the same thing as the school for painting that drips paint on the canvas. Where the organization of color was once the objective of painting, now they say, "Let's have color," and they throw the color in. The life of the mind is dead in those situations and they're profoundly unreal.

QUESTION: You speak about people learning something out of an emotional experience and then trying to figure it out. But you wouldn't go as far as Brecht has gone—to do a play without any empathic response or emotional involvement, but that would hit somewhere in between.

MR. MILLER: There are two Brechts. One is the guy who writes these essays. The other is the one who wrote the plays. Of course, the essays are much more extreme than the plays. The plays are much more empathic than he is willing to admit as an essayist. My own view is that a form ought to be distinct.

When there's a mixture of forms there's a profound disillusionment in the audience. If the idea is real objectivity, which is Brecht's idea, then it ought to be as objective as you can get. Then you end up in expressionism or some variant of it, which is what he is in. If the idea is that you just full-flush up with some emotional statement, then the romantic-realistic drama is your métier. If you respect the emotional life of the people and you believe it has as much reality as the ideology of these people, then you're in terra incognita for most of modern drama. I don't know of many examples of these dramas.

I'm in the process now of making one, and I'm the last man now to tell you how to do it. I've been four and a half years at it—on this one play—and I don't know that I've got it yet. But I believe there is a way to do it, and I intend to do it.

One rule might throw some light on the subject: The question of objective versus subjective plays is a question, to my mind, of the family and society. What basic elements are being dealt with in the play? Are they familial elements or are they social elements? The social element invariably presses toward some abstract form.

QUESTION: What happens in a play like *Awake and Sing*, which is both?

MR. MILLER: Well, then you're in trouble. One of Odets' great problems as a dramatist was that he refused to recognize that problem. Normally, we don't permit social problems to intrude upon our concepts of family. When a play does this, it cannot do it with the familiar ordinary speech of family life. So what Odets did—merely through language alone, not through a formal rearrangement of matter—he had people talk in slogans. He made little pieces of verse, quips, highly stylized measures of speech to accommodate this antipathetic family situation to a social ideology.

Another play, *Our Town*, attacked the problem from the direct opposite. *Our Town* says, "Here is a family." But if you took out society from that play, it would be the dullest thing in the world. I mean, if you put a set behind that family, there isn't a character in the play. There's no subjectivity in that play and he recognized it, because Wilder is a thinking man and a very aesthetically aware man. He was compelled to make a form that would not fight his material. He tried to elicit from the family situation the idea that, regardless of the wracks and ruins of individual fate, life is indestructible, society is indestructible, the family is indestructible. That is the idea of the play. With no characters in *Our Town*, he makes no attempt at realism. He can speak out directly, as he did in several other plays.

MR. MABLEY: *Our Town* uses the same device that you use in *A View from the Bridge*, doesn't it?

MR. MILLER: Yes, but there is an additional element in Wilder's play. My attempt was to create a certain degree of subjectivity, which he wasn't interested in. What he did was to deal with the familiar in its most abstract way. I don't think anyone would remember the name of the mother or the father or the name of the family. It's THE family, THE mother, THE father. They're objectified. They live in terms of their function rather than their personalities, which is a classic approach to drama. The reason people wept when they saw the play is because he was dealing with essentially weepy situations. They were weeping over the situations, not over the characters.

That's one answer to your question as to whether a subjective response can be gained and still create an objective design. He did it, but he sacrificed the deeper cravings of the subjective life. I think if he had started to put them in we would have seen how sentimental the play is. As soon as a character would have appeared—a real character—the design would have appeared sentimental. After all, to tell a person who is in trouble that everything's going to be all right because, even if he dies, the world is going to go on!

I do think that serious plays are not going to be written in the form that was familiar to us up through the thirties. One thing you don't have to battle for is this kind of freedom. The most difficult thing with freedom is to use it. The reason it's necessary to think about these forms is that they all afford one or another means of making meaning.

If all you're interested in is setting forth a situation for its own sake, that is to amuse for half an hour or two hours as on television, then probably the best and surest form to use is the purely realistic prose or journalistic form of play. I will never forget certain productions of Ibsen's plays that were done in the thirties. They are remarkable pieces of work. But I doubt there's going to be much energy in that form anymore. There is a remarkable amount of consciousness, of subterranean motive in the audience today that wasn't there twenty-five years ago.

Yesterday, I was standing on the corner and a cab driver let out an elderly woman right in front of me. She took two or three minutes to gather up a pair of galoshes, a raincoat, a purse, and some other objects. I was getting impatient for her to get out. She had paid the man and he looked impatient. She finally got out loaded with the stuff, walked away, and I got in.

The driver said, "You know, I picked this woman up down in the Village" (and I got this cab on 76th Street). "I took her back to Charlton Street three times. We got as close as 60th Street once. I thought then we were going to make it." I asked, "What was the matter?" He said, "Well, once she left her galoshes down there. Then we got up to 14th Street and she remembered she left her raincoat. Then she remembered she'd left something else." So I said to him," I wonder why she did that?" He said, "I guess she didn't want to leave there."

This is not a secret anymore. It is a statement Ibsen would have worked twenty minutes to make. It's an overdocumentation. We have a shorthand now. The language of psychiatry has permeated this country. If you told the driver this in academic terms, he wouldn't know what you were talking about. It was his common sense. To account for reality now requires a new level of meaning. You have to create a form in which people can say things quite as naturally as they do.

We have many species of knowledge, levels of awareness now, that they didn't have thirty, forty, fifty years ago when the realistic form was invented. You don't have to argue very long today to convince people that their social situation has an enormous bearing on their personalities. Now this was the theme of twenty-five of the great shocking plays of realism. We have to go deeper and wider now. Consequently, the form can't be the same. We are now in an era where we have enormous knowledge about the forces that make man.

It is not an arbitrary act that we get bored with realism. I wouldn't know how to write a play today in realism to really deal with practically any great issue. After twenty-five pages I'd say, yes, this is all well and good, but what about this enormous truth I can't even mention in this bloody play because these people aren't even conscious of it? So a new form has to widen the license for consciousness on the stage.

I think the culture now is at a turning point in that respect. I know that businessmen are becoming more and more aware of the value of the pure "idea man" in certain technical fields. The guy who invents something that nobody can use at any time may be of value. That is only an analogy to what is on the stage. I think that time is fast approaching when that kind of hero will not only be admired, but required. Then that will run its course. In another ten years we'll be sick and tired of people who know what's the matter with them.

QUESTION: If you throw the scenery away, you're one step in that direction. If your characters come out and talk to the audience once in a while . . .

MR. MILLER: That's one possibility. We have a necessity that they don't have much abroad. In France, or in Germany, they're perfectly content to sit in the theater from 8:30 until midnight. They regard going to the theater much as we used to regard going into the public library. You go to learn something. Now, they want to be amused, of course, entertained. But their idea of what is entertaining is quite different from ours. Let's say, they want something that's a little more austere than we're willing to take, a little bit heavier. They're perfectly willing, especially in France, to have two characters sit for fifteen minutes and talk. Theirs is an old civilization.

In my plays, there are many objectified statements. For instance, "Attention must be paid!" . . . the speech by the wife in *Death of a Salesman*, it's on the edge of being something other than what it seems to be. There are many roads to Rome and one is the highly charged emotionalism which sometimes can spurt out objective facts when nobody's looking. But, that's only one way.

What do we do with a man who commits a certain action, and as he's committing this action, he knows the root of that action is in his past? Not only does he know it, but he's incapable of undoing what he is doing now. Furthermore, he looks at it ironically. Let's say there's a man who steals. He knows why he's stealing beyond his immediate needs. How do you do that? We're all aware sometimes of a compulsion of some sort. Willy Loman does things sometimes that are compulsive actions. He has to lie and we get to know why in his present life he's being forced to lie. But what of the man who knows that? Willy doesn't know that. You get into another area. It isn't enough to flash back to his past. That's demonstrating something to us. What about him?

The manipulation of one's own past by one's own conscious mind is an area of playwriting that I don't know exists. In actual experience it goes on all the time. Many times it's disguised. But one of the things that gives vitality to an action is its repetitiveness.

QUESTION: There was a story in the *New Yorker* about a man who stole, who knew it was a crime, but he explained in great detail the excitement it gave him—going into a house and hearing the people breathing, the clocks ticking, etcetera. Perhaps that applies?

MR. MILLER: Yes. In other words, there is a sphere of knowledge which is infusing itself into reality all the time. But it's one which realism, in its standard phase, cannot deal with.

MR. MABLEY: O'Neill struggled with a great many problems like that, with masks and asides and all sorts of things.

MR. MILLER: It is a temporal problem. The mind does not function on one temporal level alone. Many of O'Neill's plays labor to bring forth a mouse. It's not his fault. He caught on to the beginning of an era which matured very rapidly and we're still right on top of the beginnings. *Mourning Becomes Electra*, some of it is mawkish. He labors to show the Oedipal situation. Today it's sold on the newsstand. It's common knowledge that the baby boy has one attitude toward the mother and a different attitude toward the father.

QUESTION: I'd like to ask about the whole Freudian level you have in your plays—like in *Death of a Salesman*. The stealing of the pen by Biff, the significance of which you said these characters don't realize. When you write a play, does an idea such as this come from your setting up the characters in an emotional way? Or did you set up the idea to illustrate the almost theoretical relationship between these characters?

<u>MR. MILLER</u>: In the psychological respect, any planning of a symbolic act didn't exist in the writing of that play. I only discovered later that there was some Freudian significance to that. If I were writing today, I would know. I didn't at the time. I have a dual view of this and always have had. As time goes on, I have tried to bring each of these two eyes, so to speak, to bear more on the center. I knew that the picture I wanted, from the point of view of the idea involved, was a reflection of what I felt about this man, and about that kind of man, and about this kind of social milieu. Its essential fruitlessness lay in the fact that the guy dies, and everybody stands around, and it's just desolate, and his life crumbles before he falls into his grave. That sense of absolute crumbling was the image I was working at, to play against a subjective feeling of the characters.

Many times I would begin a scene and it would seem to flow of itself. I don't believe that. I'm an artist. I select what I do. I have come to know that one can't undo what one knows, objectively. One must use it. If I have a consciously held idea as to the meaning of some play, of some course of action, this doesn't invalidate its subjective reality. The fact that I, the writer, happen to know something of the significance of these actions, that's organizing the contour of the action. On the other side, I am working with subjective feelings of my own which are essentially an argument. They may not follow this pattern, and in the construction of a play they may contradict it. At which point, I have to find out which has to give way.

My instinct is to say, if I wrote that so well, then the truth must be in there somewhere. If that's contradicting the contour of the story, if it's making my a priori theme seem invalid, I'd better examine that to see whether the theme is not invalid, rather than that particular turn. So it's a dialectic process. I'm trying to keep both sides vital and alive at the same time, rather than push one or the other exclusively.

<u>QUESTION</u>: When you talk about knowing a character, are you talking on a psychological level, or a social level, or both?

<u>MR. MILLER</u>: Well, I don't know people the way the wisdom of a writer is ordinarily conceived. I could draw a person fictionally and then be told something about him, as has happened to me, which I would never

have dreamed of, which was perfectly obvious to everybody else. I've lived long enough to know I don't know people.

But I think what a writer is doing basically is not knowing people in the sense that a psychoanalyst knows people, because you ought not to be interested in that kind of pragmatic view. If someone said to me, you know a man so well you would know what he would do in every situation, I'd say, no, I don't. What are you doing in a play? You're projecting a series of figures who represent in some way one of your attitudes toward the central issue in the play. Otherwise, you wouldn't select them. So they're all you in one guise or another.

Psychiatry can't do that because then it becomes a subjective operation. The analyst is not supposed to project himself into the character. All that the characters are in a play are your projections. There's an entirely different process going on. You're projecting yourself in a play.

QUESTION: Don't you think one of the reasons there are no giants may be that most writers are conditioned to think psychologically or psychoanalytically and they cut their characters down? I mean, nobody can do a noble, conscious act without someone proving they hated their mother.

MR. MILLER: There's something else working that is possibly more important, and that is the social pressures of today, which would operate on somebody who was psychoanalytically oriented or somebody who wasn't. We no longer believe in the validity of the individual will. The whole concept of a man acting alone and materially changing his environment to suit himself is reserved in our minds for ill-adjusted or delinquent or criminal types. The whole concept of a good citizen in these times is a person who adjusts himself to what we call reality, who gets along. You come upon people time after time who are perfectly good people of good will who express a helplessness about life because of the fact that they can't seem to find any leverage on it from which to exercise their will.

If you want to speak ideologically, the psychology of the time is running against the idea of the will, against the giant. We're constantly debunking alleged giants. The first thing that happens when a man goes to high office is to show how any great action on his part was really motivated by the pettiest considerations. There really wasn't even his will involved, that he was the instrument of other forces.

The number of times we can really exercise our will against the environment are few and are reserved for very few people—like artists who can create an object independently. Society is so interlocked that any individual is dependent upon a hundred and one other factors which keep him strapped to the stone. That's why we feel we are all victims. We see ourselves as being worked upon, rather than working on anything.

QUESTION: But don't you think there are people who are exerting their will but they are just not the people that playwrights are writing about?

MR. MILLER: Presumably, you're speaking about people who are involved in social reform, or in some scientific work that requires a great act of will in order to do it. An audience, in general, is distrustful of the idea that a man can make a moral decision on a large issue, excepting as a quixotic action. It goes back to *An Enemy of the People*, where Ibsen has one man who believes he's right and a whole society believes he's wrong. The whole play goes to prove that the only way anything is done is by one man alone. But look how long and how difficult it was to prove that it was possible to be that way even then. We're more comforted in a way, more consoled in our helplessness, by looking at relatively helpless people, even though the objections are usually, "I'm sick and tired of seeing this."

If you really show a hero, as I tried to do in *The Crucible*, who sees what is at stake, makes a decision, and dies for it, there's a profound distrust of the whole operation. It's truly disconcerting, because everybody is justifying his miserable existence by saying, "What can I do? That's the way it is. What do you want from me?" Everybody sees himself essentially as a victim, and there's a profound truth in that—he is!

QUESTION: About this new hero? Is he still forced to go ahead in spite of his understanding? Or is it through his understanding that he's able to exercise an act of free will?

MR. MILLER: What I'm trying to do in the play is both things. There is no such thing, in my opinion, as free will—in the sense that one can operate in a nimbus without forces. There's a point of decision in life where one, in effect, chooses to be helpless or chooses not to be helpless. For most of us, unfortunately, that point is passed without the decision having been made because there is not sufficient consciousness of what is at stake. But there are people who know that that point has arrived. In this play, I'm trying to isolate that moment when that choice is made by one of those who keeps the strength to choose, as opposed to those who want not to have it, who don't want the responsibility of any will.

QUESTION: You feel that those who have the knowledge and are able to use this in a positive way are still victims hemmed in by society?

MR. MILLER: They are all pressed by forces equally. The difference is, in this play, that certain of them know and one decides he will not be the victim. He walks into a disaster then, because people choose to be victims in order to avoid a disaster. That is the irony involved. In other words, we are what we are in order to protect ourselves.

QUESTION: I'd like to know something about the playwright as his own director.

MR. MILLER: I wish you could tell me! I directed some of my plays. I do have an actor's point of view. But it bothered me in one respect: An author is hobbled by his own knowledge. I am liable to tell the actors too much. Actors can only absorb a certain amount and they often have to be tricked into absorbing that. Certain things have to be repeated and repeated which to me, as an author, are relatively unimportant, but as part of a design are very important.

I'm also liable to lose a grip on relative emphasis. I'd be likely to play each succeeding scene with the same emphasis if I weren't careful. The whole question of rhythm of a production would suffer because there would be a steady beat. I wouldn't want to miss anything. A good director is interested in the overall design and is willing to sacrifice. And he should. I'm sure any Beethoven or Mozart would listen to certain of his symphonies and say, "My God, you went by the most beautiful passage so fast, as though it wasn't there!" He won't listen to anybody tell him it went faster so the next one could go slower.

There is also a certain literalness that authors tend to fall into. They visualize a big man and here's a little guy who's really the right guy to play the part. So, he takes the big guy, who's really very dull but looks just like the character. In other words, a certain amount of detachment, if it is accompanied by other talents, would be advisable.

MR. MABLEY: I have a question. I teach a class in playwriting. I always insist that the students read *Oedipus Rex* before we start discussing *Sales-*

man. I'm curious to know whether there was a conscious Greek pattern in the construction of *Salesman* or whether that just emerged.

MR. MILLER: There was no conscious desire to create a Greek pattern. I was very much moved by the Greek plays when I was in college and before. The thing that moves me about them is the absolute fidelity of each scene to the theme. They're written as though they were composed under a law of the Bible: "In the beginning was the Word." The word is so precious in the Greek play, it is always so useful, that under the domination of that form, one can't help but pare away any kind of writing that isn't thematically rooted.

There seems to be enormous spontaneity in *Death of a Salesman,* but it came only after some ten years of thinking about that play. It was already subconsciously organized against this theme so that almost everything is tied back to the theme; very strongly, with very clear ties. That is the Greek element in that play.

MR. MABLEY: What they have in common then is unity.

MR. MILLER: That's right. That is what is beautiful in the classic idea. You read a Greek play and it's clearly exemplifying a moral idea. The audiences came to see a moral idea. If it didn't have one, they'd ask what the hell did he write it for? I respect that aesthetic principle very much.

MR. MABLEY: I think it's evident too in *A View from the Bridge.* Very consciously there, I'm sure.

MR. MILLER: Yes, there it was because of the nature of the material. The story was actually quite Greek, or Mediterranean, and that happened to be the thematic situation. As long as I have a certain command of the theater I'd like to be able to limber it up a little bit and break down some of the conventions that oppress playwrights. There is no reason why a great play can't be written that is thirty-five to forty-five pages long. The whole convention that you have intermissions is an arbitrary thing. Greek plays have no intermissions. It's a one-act play.

Moss Hart

(1904–1961)

One rainy dawn in 1931 a young man bounced into his family's Brooklyn tenement apartment. With gleeful determination, he woke his brother and parents to inform them they were leaving their slum quarters and moving to Manhattan immediately for a better life. They were to take only one suitcase each. Soon the dazed family was in a taxi, happily headed for the glitter of Manhattan, hard times left behind.

The young man was Moss Hart, and his wildly romantic gesture came the morning after his play *Once in a Lifetime* opened to reviews that surpassed any playwright's wildest fantasies.

This dawn of fame and riches was preceded by dark days. His first play lost forty-five thousand dollars and cost Hart his job as an office boy for the producer. It was not until he was teamed with the playwright George S. Kaufman that *Once in a Lifetime* took the form that made it a hit.

Kaufman and Hart soon became one of the most beloved and successful writing duos in the history of the American stage. After mounting *Merrily We Roll Along* in 1934, the team presented a new gem, *You Can't Take It With You,* in 1937, which captured the Pulitzer Prize. They turned out yet another monster hit in 1939 with *The Man Who Came to Dinner.* (All three of their biggest stage comedies were adapted as films.)

But after the poorly received *George Washington Slept Here* in 1940, Hart and Kaufman parted. Hart went on to write and direct *Lady in the Dark* (1941), *Christopher Blake* (1946), and *The Climate of Eden* (1952).

He won a Tony Award in 1956 for his direction of Lerner and Loewe's *My Fair Lady.* (In Boston for tryouts, he issued one of American theater's classic understatements when he wrote, "I think we may have some sort of hit here.") His other directorial work included *Junior Miss* (1941) and *Anniversary Waltz* (1954). He wrote and directed *Winged Victory* (1943) and *Light Up the Sky* (1949), and produced and directed Lerner and Loewe's *Camelot* (1960).

Screenplays by Hart include *Once in a Lifetime* (1932), *Broadway Melody of 1936, Frankie and Johnnie* (1935), *George Washington Slept Here* (1942), *Winged Victory* (1944), *Lady in the Dark* (1944), *Gentleman's Agreement* (1947), *Hans Christian Andersen* (1952), and *A Star Is Born* (1954).

Hart also created librettos for musicals and reviews: *Face the Music* (1932) and *As Thousands Cheer* (1933), both with Irving Berlin; *The Great Waltz* (1934), with score by Johann Strauss Sr. and Jr.; *Jubilee* (1935), with Cole Porter; and with Kaufman, *I'd Rather Be Right* (1937).

His book *Act One: An Autobiography* was published in 1959 and filmed in 1965, four years after his death.

A New Dramatists Craft Discussion

with Moss Hart
October 4, 1956

Moss Hart is introduced by New Dramatist Sol Stein.

MR. HART: Ladies and gentlemen, I have spent most of the day trying to work on a new play, and I could not write a word, not even "cat." Each play has a particular life of its own. I think that's why playwrights never actually learn their trade, like a good cabinetmaker or shoemaker does. You keep making the same mistakes because each play has a curious life of its own.

MR. STEIN: Are there any mistakes that you don't make over and over again?

MR. HART: The only one that matters is made before you write Act I, Scene I. That's the choice of what you're going to do. It either sinks you or it doesn't. Now, I don't know why it should be, but it is a curious thing when an audience—for all the fine writing, for all the truth the play may reveal, for all the fine direction—will reject it for their own reasons.

I began by writing plays of my own. I then had a long collaboration with Mr. Kaufman, and a very happy and successful one. Then I stopped working with Mr. Kaufman and wrote a lot of plays on my own, all of which I directed. Then, in between times, I directed other people's plays.

If you're both directing and writing the play, it is a great burden. When you're on the road you watch the performance at night. Then you have to write all night. Then you have rehearsal all day, and then go back to watch the new stuff go in at night; then you write the next night! It's just a pure physical burden. I have no great illusions about myself as a director. But it's easier than going through, with someone else, that false politeness of "Don't you think that if perhaps you did 'that'…" [Laughter.]

The reason I direct other people's plays is that a playwright has a terrible hazard, the profession. The doctor may be emotionally involved with the patient. If the patient dies of course he's upset. But there are other patients. The lawyer can work on a case for two years then lose it, but he works on other cases. That isn't true of the playwright. It takes usually a year or two from the time you start to write a play to the time it gets on, and by the time you come in you are an open sore. People outside don't understand the effect of notices and the effect of failure because by the time you reach the opening, you are in a very vulnerable state.

If the play is a success, you want a breather—you don't want to go near a typewriter. If it's a failure, you can't. I am not one of the lucky ones who always has ideas. I'm always astonished and envious when they say, "I've got six plays I want to write." I'm lucky if every three or four years, to have one idea to write. Well, what do you do between-time? I suppose if you're a writer you want to write, but if you're a man of the theater, you'll do something else in the theater—direct other people's plays.

Collaboration originally just happened. I wrote *Once in a Lifetime* alone. Then Sam Harris asked me if I'd collaborate with George Kaufman on some rewriting, and I said, "Absolutely." We stayed together for ten years.

QUESTION: The first play you directed was your own play, wasn't it?

MR. HART: The first play I directed was *As Thousands Cheer.* Yes.

QUESTION: Before that, had you directed any other plays?

MR. HART: Not professionally. I was trying to be a playwright. In order to evolve a way of life so I could find the time to write, I did summers as a social director, which involved putting on plays. In winters I directed plays at night for little theaters so I had the days free.

QUESTION: Mr. Hart, it's often said that the playwright-director (in directing his own play) has shortcomings because he is too close to his play.

MR. HART: I think that's valid. A play of mine suffered from my own direction.

QUESTION: What was that?

MR. HART: *The Climate of Eden.* After being in the theater all day and watching the performance, you cannot be as fresh as you could be if you were just rewriting. I think directors in our theater today are a highly overrated commodity. Now if it wasn't on tape, I'd deny I said this. [Laughter.] This applies to myself as well as to everybody else.

QUESTION: There are certain directors who are famous for their "director's touch." Do you think a play which has this "director's touch" is a valid thing, because it may not necessarily parallel or enforce the playwright's ideas?

MR. HART: The terrible thing about these talks is that everything said about theater can be refuted in the next breath. It's why I say you never learn how to write plays correctly, no matter how long you write them. Now, sometimes the play gains by that directorial touch—even though it is twisted out of shape a little. And sometimes the playwright's intent may not emerge as he wanted it to, but if you think about it, the same director who was so highly praised one season for his touch will then be damned the next season with "This is terribly dull."

It is usually the play. Now, you must remember that direction is not just telling the actors not to bump into each other. It is a very creative problem. As a playwright I object to the place a director is assuming in the theater. It is a secondary creative art, and they are gradually usurping some of the rights of the playwright.

QUESTION: In Louis Kronenberger's book *Company Manners* he stated that even though a play might be ruined or improved by a director, one of the things sometimes missing is the validity of the individual talent. How much better to see a less-than-brilliant production of one man's vision than an amalgamation of a number of visions which may not necessarily coincide. What are your views?

MR. HART: Again, it depends on the play. Some plays emerge full-blown and ready for production. I always work with a playwright for at least four months before rehearsal. Actually, the creative part of directing is working with the playwright months before you go into rehearsal. Also scenery, costumes—let me give you one instance: *My Fair Lady.* We had worked on the script, and I had okayed all of Cecil Beaton's costume design, but I said to the producers and the authors, "Please look at the plates. I just okayed the bill and it's very expensive." They said, "No, no, we trust your judgment." "I don't want you to trust my judgment. It's something like seventy-five thousand dollars for these costumes, and I'd like you to have a look at them."

They didn't want to, but they did. That evening we met by accident and to my surprise, they hadn't liked a couple of the sets of costumes. One set of them was the Ascot scene. I thought it was Cecil Beaton's most brilliant contribution. They gave their reasons, but I said, "Well, I must overrule you. You got me for my mistakes as well as for my virtues, and I insist they go through." Now, it turned out I was right. It happened at that moment that I had a great sense of security. At another moment, I might have said, "All right, let's change it!" But you know, on such things are hits made.

That is one of the contributions of a strong director—I don't mean an overriding director. There must be someone in authority. Preferably the author, but if he's a young author he hasn't the authority to control a production. It's been my experience the whole secret to success in a tryout or out of town, is to get control *early*. I've sometimes gone to a play in New Haven that needed work. Four or six weeks later they'd come in with changes made, but not with what *should* have been done.

Every time, I found that whoever was in control, author, producer, or director, had not got control early. Remember when you're dealing with shows, you're dealing not with that script but with personalities—the star, the author, director, producers. In a musical comedy as big as *My Fair Lady*, it can be catastrophic unless you have an iron control.

QUESTION: Some of us here have had the experience of trying to cowrite with somebody else. Most of these turn out to be unsuccessful because we don't know how to write with somebody. Could we eavesdrop in on one of your early meetings with Mr. Kaufman—in discussing a play you wished to write?

MR. HART: I guess that we hit it off. We thought more or less alike, with a satirical attitude, for want of a better term. The kind of plays we were doing were very much akin. I can only tell you that Mr. Kaufman sat at the typewriter, while I sat in a chair or walked or paced—I'm talking about the actual writing of the play.

MR. STEIN: Can we start with Alexander Woollcott [referring to *The Man Who Came to Dinner*]—what happened from that time on?

MR. HART: Woollcott was playing *Wine of Choice* in Philadelphia, and I had a farm in Bucks County. Uninvited, he just popped in. [Laughter.] I had other guests for the weekend and he was insulting to them. He made the weekend an absolute hell. Of course, he had to go back Monday night to Philadelphia. He asked me to go with him and I, of course, would have gone to China to get him out of the house.

On the way back from Philadelphia I stopped by George Kaufman's house nearby. He said, "How was the weekend?" and I said, "Just hideous—absolutely awful!" I told him some of the things and it crossed my mind—Woollcott was a very fat man—my God! If he had tripped on the stairs and broken his leg, I don't know what I'd have done! [Laughter.] We looked at each other and said, "There it is!" [Laughter.] Now, that was the happy way. But most of the time we dug for ideas.

MR. STEIN: Do you talk out your story lines together and take notes on it?

MR. HART: In those days, we would decide on an idea that would please us both, and that was the only time we differed. But when we finally decided, we'd sit down and do a kind of shorthand. We'd write the whole first act in a kind of staccato on half a page. The same thing with the second and third acts. Then we'd sit down and write Act 1, Scene 1. If George thought a line I was suggesting wasn't funny, it would never occur to me to say, "Yes, it *is* funny." We'd strive for a better one.

MR. STEIN: It'd have to pass the test of both of you.

MR. HART: It has always escaped me how one of the authors can do a section and come back to his partner and go over it together. I wouldn't understand that, because there's a curious inner symphonic beat to the play. So that one line is an actual crescendo to the next line . . .

QUESTION: How does one determine in the musical what section is lyric and what sections are spoken?

MR. HART: Well, in the musicals I've done, I've worked directly with the composer. After the idea is blocked out, you say, "There should be a song here and a song there," and you write up to it.

QUESTION: Sir, your point earlier about the die being cast before the play actually has even started, does that have any bearing on the out-of-town work?

MR. HART: I've seen, and have myself, broken my back and my heart working on plays and gotten them within an inch of being as good as they possibly could be in terms of rewrite. And they failed. I've seen plays with enormous holes in them tried out of town, not fixed as they should be, and they've been successes.

It's that curious idiot genius an audience has that works both ways. They detect falsity. En masse in the theater, you've seen them reject the spurious in a play. But they also react in the other way and accept something. Every season there are one or two plays that we don't understand why they are successes, but they are! And that's why I say the die is usually cast.

QUESTION: Do you very often leave a finished script and then rewrite it? Or do you try to move into production?

MR. HART: The ideal thing would be if you finish a play, put it away for a month, two months, three months, six months if possible, and look at it again. I've never done that. What usually happens is in the middle of the second act, a theater has been booked. [Laughter.] This is really true, and I think it is foolish. It would be wonderful to have that six months.

I suppose it is pure vanity. I cannot wait to see this brilliant thing I've done on the stage and receive those wonderful notices. It doesn't always turn out that way!

MR. STEIN: We in this room have heard it said frequently that if you've got a good play it'll go and if it's a bad play it won't, and the critics have very little to do with it. Do you think that's true of *My Fair Lady*?

MR. HART: No, I don't think it's true of any play. If *My Fair Lady* had gotten bad notices, I'd expect a rough time in spite of all the out-of-town reports. Maybe we'd have fought our way through and gotten an audience. Actually, I believe the critics are not only honest, but very fair. The terrible thing about the theater is that sometimes you get less than you deserve and sometimes you get more than you deserve.

QUESTION: How many of the ideas are rejected by you because you feel they will not be a hit?

MR. HART: I'm talking in terms of a playwright's—if you'll forgive the word—integrity. What we're talking about is not in terms of the Broadway commercial theater, but the play you want to do. I've found that no play idea is ever accidental. You may have bad luck with it, but a play is the expression of an author's particular personality at that particular time. As he grows, his ideas—his plays—change.

One of the tough things about our theater is that it doesn't allow room for mistakes. An interesting playwright should have an audience who goes to see his plays whether or not it's that box-office hit. We know that isn't true, but it's sad because how else can you grow if you can't learn from your mistakes? What you're asking is, "Do you reject the idea sometimes because it hasn't the possibilities of a hit?"

QUESTION: You yourself have a very deep desire to do the right play or the . . .

MR. HART: To be absolutely honest, maybe sometimes one does. When you're writing those first few plays, there's a kind of innocence. Once you've had success, it's very hard to recapture that innocence. Not only do you *not* like to fail, there's a certain standard you're held to. Also, by the time you've done a few plays, you know the toll each play takes. You know before you sit down to write how bloody tough it is. You know about that conspiracy that starts to defeat this play just as it leaves the typewriter. [Laughter.]

You sometimes say to yourself, "God, I wish I didn't have to write this particular play. I wish I had a more commercial idea." This doesn't happen very often, because I'm talking about playwrights who respect their craft. If it were possible to sit down and write a hit, they would all do it.

QUESTION: I know the critics like to talk about the theater as opening up new vistas and that we're getting away from naturalism.

MR. HART: Well, one of my difficulties has been, I haven't always hewn to the line. Critics don't like you to get a little big for yourself by writing a wide range of plays. *Christopher Blake* to *Lady in the Dark* to *The Climate of Eden*—they didn't remain in one category. One should be allowed to grow. One of the reasons I couldn't write "and" or "cat" this afternoon was because I think it has a chance, even now, of going down like the SS *Andrea Doria*. [Laughter.]

As far as fads or conventions are concerned, the so-called mood play has certain advantages. There was a time when the verse play had a great vogue. Maxwell Anderson. I thought one of Max's great mistakes was to stop writing in verse and write in prose.

QUESTION: What happens to the ideas you don't use, Mr. Hart?

MR. HART: Unfortunately, I never have that many to choose from! Now this one I'm working on is an idea I've had for two or three years, which I'd rather not write, but now I feel impelled to write it. It may be a roaring failure, but I can't help it. I never have those *two* ideas. I wish I did.

QUESTION: Some people maintain that *Waiting for Godot* was an important play, and that this is really the trend that theater is going to take.

MR. HART: *Waiting for Godot* was the Elvis Presley of the season. [Laughter.] I was not bored by the first act. I thought it spun out. But I'll tell you, it reminded me that in the twenties, when I came to the theater, it was in a much more flourishing state than it is now. But it was a much more professional state. There were the special matinees. O'Neill was first done on Broadway at a special matinee.

In those days, the theater was full of *Waiting for Godot's*. I'm ashamed to say it, but this seemed very old hat. It escaped me just the way Mr. Presley does. [Laughter.]

MR. STEIN: Is there some special reason why a very excellent writer of comedy—musical comedy—would want to write a different kind of play?

MR. HART: A first-rate comedy is a wonderful way of saying certain things you could not even say in a tragedy. It wasn't that I felt by writing comedies that I wasn't a serious writer. If you are to grow as a playwright, then you change. If you don't change, you don't grow.

For instance, I thought Saroyan, at one time, had a great gift for the theater. It was strange, moving, and touching. But he kept writing the same play, the *same play!* That was unfortunately true of Odets. I don't think Mr. Paddy Chayefsky has written a complete play as yet. He has a fine instinct for the theater. To me, he writes a series of vignettes. They never seem to climax. They're never a sustained play with the people drawn in full dimension.

The fooling thing is that they're terribly effective on television because television is a kind of crystallization of a moment. But when I saw *Middle of the Night* I didn't admire it as being a play. I don't mean this in a terribly derogatory sense, but that whole kind of television playwriting is terribly effective on TV. At least Mr. Tennessee Williams writes a full-bodied play.

If plays consisted of vignettes and moods, we'd all be rich. One of the reasons playwriting pays so well—the rewards are so great—is that not many people can do it.

One of the depressing things about playwriting is that the ability to write dialogue is pennies from heaven. Without it, all the technical things in the world don't mean anything. There are two kinds of dialogue. There is what I call visual dialogue. You know, if you read a Hemingway book, that dialogue is not only expert, but true—to the eye. But try to put that on the stage and have actors speak it; it would seem false as hell.

About three years ago, I read O'Neill's *Beyond the Horizon*, one of the great plays of my youth, and I was staggered by how bad it was. I just couldn't believe that it changed, single-handed, the whole American theater. Recently I read *Long Day's Journey into Night*. He writes like a butcher! It's staggering that this man—a great playwright—has so little imagery, so little poetry, so little command of English.

But by the time you finish *Long Day's Journey into Night*, it is of enormous power. He violates every rule of playwriting. It's very repetitive. One person says, "This is what happened to me," and in the next scene that person listens and the other person says, "Yes, and this is what happened to me." But by the end of the play it doesn't matter. It's because O'Neill was convinced early of his own greatness. He couldn't have written the way he did unless he was deeply convinced that he was a great playwright. By God, it matters. [Laughter.] Now, as you know by my report of this afternoon's work, I'm not suffering from the same conviction.

QUESTION: Can the literary content be so unimportant? Can you stand O'Neill against playwrights who do have a command of language?

MR. HART: You can because you can't question the emotion he engenders. I was just bewailing the fact that this great American dramatist did not have as much poetry and imagery as I'd like to see him have. He was a sparse writer in terms of words as weapons.

QUESTION: Do you feel that verbal pyrotechnics or poetic dialogue will save the dramatist who's deficient on technique and the ability to construct a play?

MR. HART: The two go hand in hand. If you haven't got that curious ability to write dialogue that actors seem to be speaking for the first time and making up as they go along, all the technique in the world doesn't matter.

QUESTION: I meant the converse of that. Very often we hear or read a play and say, "Gee, wonderful lines! The guy writes very well, but there's no play here. The structure is lacking." Do you think verbal excellence is enough?

MR. HART: Not for a long career in the theater.

QUESTION: Concerning the lack of a place to make mistakes in the theater: It sounds terrible to say this, but there seemed to me a kind of curious flaw in *My Fair Lady*. It's the first-act curtain. One anticipates the act's ending about ten minutes before it does. Then those wonderful two little men jump out on stage and hold you there for the next scene, and then you get the first-act curtain.

MR. HART: Oh, you mean, we're going to go to the ball . . . I'll tell you exactly what happened. We threw out, in New Haven, a ballet and four songs. It was a great deal too long. As *always* happens, the chorus couldn't make the costume change, the stagehands couldn't make the change. You see, those two big revolving stages could not be made in time. They had to get out that big set—the study—with just the curtain drawn. We just couldn't. We had provided for it in the original thing, with the ballet and the . . .

QUESTION: Where did the ballet come?

MR. HART: The ballet came in Higgins' study. Rex Harrison danced in it, and danced very well. But it had to come out. Then that scene where he takes her to the ball was written on the road. But in order to get from his study scene into the ballroom, there was nothing we could do but let it stand there as you've wisely pointed out, and hope they'd forgive us if the rest of the show was good enough, and they did.

QUESTION: Sir, regarding *Light Up the Sky*, there was a fault in that play that ran through the whole backbone, and I wonder if a discussion of that might be edifying—problems of structure?

MR. HART: My original notes for *Light Up the Sky* were as an allegory. I was trying to say that people behave terribly well in crises and the moment the crisis is over, they behave miserably.

What I was trying to do was an allegory on the United Nations. Now this seems very far removed, but you asked the question so I . . . [Laughter.] The idea was that these people had gotten together and behaved better than usual—these rather sleazy theatrical people—because they were all dedicated to this play. But the minute it got bad notices, they fell apart and behaved terribly. Well, when we opened in New Haven the first act played wonderfully. The audience thought this is going to be a very funny theatrical comedy. The second-act curtain rose, and some of my finest writing was spoken on that stage. And they just rejected it. They were angry; they were mad; they felt they had been led down the garden path because they had come to see a comedy and the first act *was* comedy. In the second act I was getting a helluva lot of things off my chest, and they were furious!

The second and third acts played deadly. Deadly. I had to make a terrible choice. Either I said, "This is the play I want to write, and that's the way it's going to be—whether they like it or not!" or, "I can salvage this. I can say, 'They're right and I'm wrong; and I've done it badly.'" So we booked two extra weeks on the road, and except for about four lines of the opening of the second act, I rewrote two solid acts.

QUESTION: Couldn't you have rewritten the first and kept your other two?

MR. HART: Wasn't possible, for, as you can guess, the thought crossed my mind. [Laughter.]

QUESTION: I thought since it was a comedy, you could cheat.

MR. HART: I suppose I took the cowardly choice, really. But it's the choice I made. Absolutely open-eyed and coldly while I was watching that first act I said, "There is a chance for this play to be a hit in these terms. Those are the terms I led them to believe they were going to get."

Then I fooled them. If you want to write that serious play, write it serious. Don't try to do what I did—try to have your cake and eat it. We rewrote two whole new acts, and it damn near killed me.

QUESTION: I read *How Not to Write a Play* by Walter Kerr. He refers to play after play which has the third-act summary, the summarizing of the whole theme in the dialogue of one or two characters.

MR. HART: It's usually wrong. Arthur Miller never said once in *Death of a Salesman*, "This is what this play is about." He never summed it up at the end, really. Nor did Williams in *A Streetcar Named Desire*. It's a mistake to me when you have to.

QUESTION: Would you say there are certain types of plays that an author should almost welcome an assured director's touch? For instance, comedy, which on paper is so often nothing, and then that wonderful transformation . . .

MR. HART: The ideal direction to me is direction that you don't really notice. The play looks undirected. You mentioned something about Actors Studio—well, you can sometimes detect Actors Studio playing on the stage. They're little isolated islands of rebellion against the other actors. [Great laughter.] To me, that's bad acting, just like the director who's so anxious to leave his imprint.

Comedy is a very special cup of tea. You have to be terribly surefooted. Most of the directorial touches are not done in comedy. They put that touch in the serious play, because you are shown up in comedy very quickly.

QUESTION: I want to know how you approach directing straight actors in a musical. Had Rex Harrison ever done a musical before?

MR. HART: No. Never had.

QUESTION: It's a remarkable job he does. I noticed the broad playing of the consultation scene between the girl and the mother. It couldn't possibly be done in a regular play this way. Yet it worked within the musical comedy . . .

MR. HART: I must take a little bow for that, then. Since you brought it up, thank you! [Laughter.] The original scene, as you know [the tea party], took place in his mother's home. I was determined that I wasn't going to do that tea scene again. I don't want to hear those tea cups clatter. We then decided to do it in Ascot, at the races, to get out of the house. We'd been in Higgins' study for a long time. Now the minute we did it at Ascot, I thought, "What better way of doing it than to stylize it?" Move everyone straight across the stage as you would in *The Importance of Being Earnest.* Or if you were doing Restoration comedy, you would stylize it. So far as Harrison was concerned, he was just as scared of singing as I was scared of directing Shaw. He had never sung, so [laughter] we had that in common.

QUESTION: Mr. Hart, do you think that in writing a musical comedy you automatically assume certain things? For instance, you bring the boy and the girl on the stage and the audience assumes that these are the people who are going to be the lovers.

MR. HART: That's true. Just think of what the audience does at a musical which they wouldn't do at a play. Suddenly two people burst into song, then stop and go on with the story. You accept this and believe it. Think of what a strange convention that is. You couldn't possibly do that any other way. You do have a kind of shorthand. On the other hand, the game just refutes everything. In *My Fair Lady* there's a scene of dialogue which lasts twenty-eight minutes with not a note sung. In the study, just pure Shaw. So, one can only say write [laughter] just the way you feel.

QUESTION: I hate to hammer this point, but did you take the twenty-eight minutes of dialogue and play it as though a song *were* about to be sung? In other words, did you keep in a style . . .

MR. HART: No. You see, this twenty-eight minutes comes very early in the play. By the tea scene at Ascot I was able to live a little dangerously. But in that first twenty-eight minutes, as you know, we played it pure Shaw. There's an interesting thing that goes for plays as well as musicals. If you have the courage to create your own authority, ultimately, they'll accept it. In *The King and I,* and in most of Rodgers and Hammerstein's stuff, they had the courage of creating their own authority. There was no dance in *The King and I* until the second act, and there were long, long stretches of dialogue.

QUESTION: How successful can a writer be in picking the character that is not a part of his own personality?

MR. HART: Just as good as his talent is, really.

QUESTION: Can you really pick something that isn't a part of yourself?

MR. HART: Oh, God, I should think so, yes. [Laughter.] Otherwise it circumscribes the sort of play you're going to be able to write! [Laughter.] No, I think the whole aspect of characterization is the playwright's *imagination* in terms of character, rather than what he knows.

QUESTION: In the light of *My Fair Lady*, would you have any predictions as to how far musicals could go?

MR. HART: Well, there's no question in my mind that the public, in general, would rather see a musical. The public's taste is first musical, then comedy, and then if they have to [laughter] . . . I mean this seriously. If they really have to—in order to be able to say, "Yes, I saw *Death of a Salesman*, yes, I saw *Streetcar*"—if they have to—they will go to see that serious play or tragedy. Actually, you get a better shake of the dice with a musical. The chances of it being successful are a little bit better than they are for anything else.

QUESTION: This is "which came first, the chicken or the egg?" In working with a musical what is it—the lyrics first . . . ?

MR. HART: Everyone works differently. Lerner and Loewe wrote the entire score of *My Fair Lady* before they touched the book—which drove me crazy, but they did. When I did *As Thousands Cheer* with Irving Berlin, we went away together for eight weeks and bit by bit constructed the show. Song by song, sketch by sketch—same thing with Cole Porter. We took a trip around the world, which is a strange way to do a show. I was the fellow, when I first heard "Begin the Beguine," said, "It's no good. It's too long!" [Laughter.]

QUESTION: How much do you think the lavishness of a show contributes to the success?

MR. HART: Well, lavish or not, the costs are enormous. The expense when things are *wrong* in a musical is quadrupled, compared to a play. If something's wrong with a play, it's the poor author who sits in his bedroom and rewrites. But with a musical, sets and costumes come out, a new song goes in. They're enormously expensive. I just wish that the theater weren't as suicidal, economically. You're all very courageous people. I don't know how in hell you're going to get the apprenticeships people used to get—things are so difficult economically in the theater. In spite of it, people who can write plays do get produced.

There's a kind of rough justice about theater. If you have a play that's good, by God, red carpets are put down and doors fly open. It gets done. That still is true. It just is tougher in this kind of hit-flop theater we're in to learn the actual job of playwriting. You literally have to go on the road, doing it under pressure, finding out for yourself. I don't think that all the books on playwriting are a good substitute.

MR. STEIN: Thank you very much. [Applause.]

PHOTOGRAPH COURTESY OF WESLEYAN UNIVERSITY CINEMA ARCHIVES.

Elia Kazan

(1909–)

The son of Greek immigrants who had lived in Turkey, Elia Kazan was raised in New Rochelle, New York, and attended Williams College. Fascinated by the stage, he moved on to the Yale Drama School, where he met his first wife, the writer Molly Day Thatcher. In 1931 he joined the pioneering Group Theatre, working first as a stage manager, before gaining recognition as an actor for his performance in Clifford Odets' *Waiting for Lefty.*

Two of his earliest directorial efforts, Irwin Shaw's *Quiet City* and Robert Ardrey's *Thunder Rock,* both achieved less than hoped for. But Kazan's direction of Thornton Wilder's *The Skin of Our Teeth* (1942) and *Harriet,* starring Helen Hayes (1943), pushed him into the forefront of American directors.

These triumphs were followed in 1947 by the staging of his first Tony winner, Arthur Miller's *All My Sons,* then Tennessee Williams' *A Streetcar Named Desire,* starring Jessica Tandy and Marlon Brando. In 1949 Kazan won his second Tony, for Miller's *Death of a Salesman.* He enjoyed similar success in Hollywood, where he won the first of his Oscars for *Gentleman's Agreement* in 1947. That same year, he, Bobby Lewis, and Cheryl Crawford founded the Actors Studio, which made famous in America the acting techniques and methods of Konstantin Stanislavsky and the Moscow Art Theater, and which has served as a training ground for a host of talent.

Kazan won his second Oscar in 1954 for *On the Waterfront*. In 1957 he took a Tony for his direction of William Inge's *The Dark at the Top of the Stairs*. Other popular stage hits he directed include Robert Anderson's *Tea and Sympathy* (1953), Williams' *Cat on a Hot Tin Roof* (1955) and *Sweet Bird of Youth* (1959), and Miller's *After the Fall* (1964). In 1958, he directed Archibald MacLeish's *JB,* which won the Pulitzer Prize.

Among Kazan's major films are *A Tree Grows in Brooklyn* (1945), *Panic in the Streets* (1950)*, A Streetcar Named Desire* (1951), *Viva Zapata!* (1951), *East of Eden* (1955), *Baby Doll* (1956), *A Face in the Crowd* (1957), *Wild River* (1960), and *Splendor in the Grass* (1961).

He turned to writing at an age when many are contemplating retirement and produced a best-selling novel, *The Arrangement* (1967), as well as *The Assassins* (1972), *The Understudy* (1974), *Act of Love* (1978), *The Anatolian* (1982), and an autobiography, *Elia Kazan: A Life* (1988).

A NEW DRAMATISTS CRAFT DISCUSSION

with Elia Kazan
April 9, 1957

George Hamlin is moderator.

MR. HAMLIN: Let's open with questions.

QUESTION: What happens when you get a script that excites you?

MR. KAZAN: I make arrangements to do it as fast as I can. But it's hard to tell what excites you. It varies in different periods of your life. I've often thought my tastes were rather narrow and uncatholic, but I have done a fair variety of stuff. It seems to me increasingly to be coming out more and more the same. It's a problem I have in my own work; this thing of repeating myself. I suppose authors have the same problem, or painters or anybody. I tend toward subjects that I know something about or an examination of a field of experience in which I've participated. I really try to read something just as a fellow reading something, and if it does excite me, I try to make arrangements to do it. Of course, it must be made under favorable conditions.

QUESTION: Does reading something along historical lines ever excite you?

MR. KAZAN: It never has. Historical is already my own youth now. [Laughter.] I read this book by Arthur Schlesinger Jr. last week and I was very excited by that. When I read again what Hoover said and what Coolidge said, their remarks both shocked me and gave my memory a tremendous jolt, and that did excite me. That's historical.

QUESTION: I mean historical à la *Crucible* historical.

MR. KAZAN: *Crucible* historical? I read *The Crucible*. I didn't see it. It had contemporary references, but when I read it, it seemed remote to me. I rarely have been excited by that sort of thing. But I was once on the Goldwyn lot when they were doing a picture based on New York City in 1600. Well, after you've done a few pictures in Hollywood you get to know all the extras. This fellow came up to me and said, "Don't you remember me?" and I said, "Oh, my God, what are you doing?" He said, "I'm in this picture about the Dutch in New York City." And I said, "How's it going?" and he said, "There's never been a success in this costume!" [Laughter.]

QUESTION: Mr. Kazan, how did you feel when you first got hold of the script for *Camino Real*?

MR. KAZAN: I never got hold of it. What happened was we got hold of it at Actors Studio. We were looking for little experimental things to do and I did a scene from it—the Gypsy's daughter scene. I did that with Eli [Wallach], and a little girl named Nancy Franklin, and Adelaide Klein. When we did it I showed it to Williams, and he got very stimulated by the possibilities.

QUESTION: It wasn't his scene originally?

MR. KAZAN: Oh, he wrote it. It was about a forty-minute play originally.

QUESTION: *Camino Real* seems to be the farthest you've managed to reach in getting out of the usual stuff.

MR. KAZAN: Yeah, I welcomed that. As a matter of fact, I wish I had something like that to do over. I thought I did that too heavily and too realistically.

QUESTION: When you take a script like *Camino*, which doesn't seem to have an obvious structure, how do you evaluate it?

MR. KAZAN: It's awfully hard to have a success of a play that's not successful on its own terms. *Camino Real* has a story. The symbology of the story is not concrete, not realistic, but it has a story. A man comes into an imaginary place and finds that he's doomed to die there, and so he does, under imaginary circumstances and with imaginary trimmings. I think that in this case you can say it has a story and not a plot. Some plot, some plotting, some sense of suspense created as you're led to believe a certain thing is going to happen, but it has more of a story than a plot. I enjoyed it, though.

As I said, I'd like to do more like that. You had to pull it out a little bit. But if you look at it carefully, Tennessee is writing about his own experience in the world. His own sense of isolation, his own sense of terror. He's surrounded by hostile forces that are antagonistic to a person like himself. He's affirming the validity of the sensory-sensual life and the purity of the vagabond, non-middle-class man. He's writing almost as directly as he does in his realistic plays.

As a matter of fact, some of the scenes are more real than some of his realistic plays, but they don't purport to be real. Sometimes, when he writes about an absolutely real thing like the South, you say, "Christ, that's not the South!" Your sense of reality's offended; but in that play, often it wasn't.

QUESTION: What is the difference in attack in a mood show and in a show full of story? In other words, how would you place the emphasis?

MR. KAZAN: A director gets a tremendous sense of relief when he gets a strong story. In a sense, he can *lie* on the story, he can rest on it. He doesn't feel he has to work hard. The story sustains him, especially if it has a plot. You don't feel you have to bolster it up every moment; rather, you underplay the effects. In a mood show you're trying to be entrancing or entertaining from moment to moment. You constantly feel you must make each moment so delightful, or so beautiful, or so funny, or so something.

QUESTION: In *Tea and Sympathy*, which was the case?

MR. KAZAN: Oh, that's a beautifully put together piece of construction.

QUESTION: When you first got it, was it well put together then?

MR. KAZAN: Oh, God, yes. We did about two or three weeks' work. Mainly what we did was make the father and the husband less villainous, but the essential structure was there when I got it. The climax was there. My whole effort in that play was to control myself, just mute it and let the story come through. Let the characters come through as real and unstrained. I tried to play that in the mood of Chopin. Quiet, muted, understressed, and continuously flowing.

QUESTION: Is there a point where you could say a play's overconstructed or constructed so well, so pat, that it kills the kind of life it has?

MR. KAZAN: One important problem in playwriting is to get real characters and still get construction. Very often, when you make all your choices because the construction is affected, you tend to obliterate real character values—the complexity of the character values. Is that what you mean?

QUESTION: Yes, I felt that about *Tea and Sympathy.* So pat—so clear! Did you work with the playwright before rehearsals started?

MR. KAZAN: Yes. We did three or four weeks' hard work. We had a general discussion or two first, mainly about the father being too much of a heavy and especially about the husband being loaded in the wrong way. It made the drama less because the husband was so heavy; it seemed a set-up thing. Once Bob [Anderson] agreed to this generalization, he went away and then came back with bits here and bits there and cuts. You know Bob. He's a terribly methodical man and he brings four copies of everything. [Laughter.]

But he worked everything out, and gradually, by this very subtle, very careful, terribly conscientious work, he swung the value over to an extent. I don't think he swung it quite as much as he might have. I think way back in his mind—since the source of the play is a creative one out of his own life—he had a grudge against the husband and some natural enlistment with himself and the boy. He never entirely overcame it.

QUESTION: Just how far do you go as a director in suggesting changes in the domain—if there is a domain—of the playwright?

MR. KAZAN: Well, there is a domain of the playwright, but I don't give a damn how far I infringe. It's for the playwright to protect himself. I say absolutely everything I feel, but I don't say it in a loud voice or in a bullying manner. I say it repeatedly until I'm either heard or drowned out—and that can be done very easily.

A playwright can say, "That's the way I want it." He's protected by the Dramatists Guild and he's also protected by my concern for him. If I really can't convince him, I can't. But I do make an effort to tell him exactly what I think is wrong. And I do it very particularly, do it at length and in detail. I also try to make suggestions. But I do make suggestions of the kind of things that will fix the script—that might give the kind of value I think needed. But truly, when you take on a play as a director, you're responsible for it. If you like it enough to do it, you've got to believe it can be successful before an audience. That doesn't mean a commercial success, but that it can communicate. You're engaged to deliver the author's message to the audience.

It's only fair and right, when you undertake a thing, that you tell the author what your reservations are and what your critical feelings are—and I do before I start. I say, "Look, I like your play very much and I'd like to do it. But I want you to know exactly how I feel." The author can always say, "Look, that's the most I can do. I can't feel it more than that." People have said that. Tennessee has many times.

Sometimes I make mistakes. I made a mistake with Arthur Miller once. We cut out some scenes at the beginning of Act 2 of *Death of a Salesman.* My wife, Molly, read the rewrite and said we'd spoiled it. Miller and I were convinced she was right and we put the scenes back. Sometimes you do make mistakes, but there's no use pussyfooting; the relationship is too critical and too vital. You're really there to say what you think, to give the author the benefit of your complete candid opinions.

QUESTION: There are other problems with, say, *Baby Doll,* when you adapt it for the movies. From what I gather, there were many problems that came up.

MR. KAZAN: Oh, yeah. There were many problems that came up there. The main problem there was that we didn't really work together enough. Tennessee didn't want to make a movie of it. He says how much he admires the motion picture form, but he's a playwright.

QUESTION: Do you think it hurts playwrights to write motion pictures? Or television?

MR. KAZAN: In a way I do. They're different forms.

QUESTION: What are some of the distinctive differences?

MR. KAZAN: In the other media, you're speaking through pictures. That's a bromide, but it's absolutely true. You're saying a hell of a lot of it through pictures, and suggesting a lot through pictures. The play is a literary form no matter how dramatized it is. You're speaking through words and action, of course. I always hope in the movies that I'll end up with an eighty-page shooting script. In essence, I guess this is what you tell pupils: A movie should tell a story without words; you ought to be able to watch it without words and still get the same story out of it. The picture should tell it all.

QUESTION: When you're getting ready to go into rehearsal of a play, how much discussion do you have with a playwright on interpretation?

MR. KAZAN: My advice to you is to get hold of your director, go off somewhere for a few weeks, and talk and talk and talk, so that you know exactly what he has in mind and he knows exactly what you have in mind. Don't have any arguments after you start. It's unforgivable for a playwright to say to a director, or a director to say to a playwright, "Well, I always thought that . . ." You do have that time before and you should have a complete understanding as to goal, attention, end, content, theme, style—everything! Just talk it out.

Read the play aloud to each other, if necessary. Talk about things that are parallel, that are suggested; talk about the kind of props. Almost anything is important. Talk about what people should wear. Argue back and forth, but become as close as you can to being one. Then at least you have frames of reference. The most ghastly thing that can happen in theater is to find that in the third or fourth week you have a basic disagreement. It happened to me once, and I'll never allow it to happen again. It throws off the whole production. I didn't talk the thing out honestly enough with the author.

QUESTION: Would you rather not have the author there while you're rehearsing?

MR. KAZAN: Sometimes you want him there more often than other times. I'll give you several examples. Take the movie I just did. A movie script is essentially an unfinished piece of work because so much of it depends on picture and improvisation. You have no out-of-town road trip. You haven't even had a reading of most of the scenes. So much depends on what you're doing on the set every day that ideally an author should be there continuously. I've only had that once, and it's damn helpful; it was just now with Budd Schulberg on *A Face in the Crowd*. He was there just about every day. It's helpful because each day you're producing a minute or two minutes or three minutes of film for the finished picture.

Now in a play, of course, it's not always necessary to have the author there. Some authors are worriers who come in a lot. Tennessee always comes in the afternoon, and if things are going well, he'll sit there laughing. If things aren't going well, he'll go next door and have a drink, disappear and come back the next day. He's quite reactive about it and he's absolutely brilliant in his perceptions. But sometimes he's helpful and sometimes he's not. Most authors haven't a sense of stages. I still remember Arthur Miller after seven or eight days of *Death of a Salesman* walking up and down, his fists clenched, face tensed, body like a ramrod, saying, "When are they going to learn the lines?" [Laughter.] As if that was the problem.

Thornton Wilder is terribly exact about everything he does. He is very thorough and methodical. He showed up every third day and sat there all day. Well, it's kinda nice, you know. You have two days . . . [laughter] and on the third day he's able to see something new and you get a reaction to the progress of your work. But at the same time, if he's not there often, it's really dangerous because you may be going off. The bond should really be a hand-in-glove one.

QUESTION: What do you think about the playwright as the director?

MR. KAZAN: I don't really like it. It's hard enough to do a good job under the best of circumstances, but if you have a director who's in sympathy with you, you both see closely on the thing. He's tough on you and you're tough on him, and you get a lot by talking together and reacting to each other. It is a good two-man job. There's also something about handling actors that's a special craft. It's a profession of its own.

QUESTION: Frankly, I'm speaking about myself. [Laughter.] I've had experiences as an actor and as a director, and directed my own plays, and so on. Now, if the playwright has had some experience as a director or an actor so that he understands the problems he faces, don't you think it's possible to get rid of the director who is nothing but a middleman between what the writer created and what comes off on the stage?

MR. KAZAN: If the director's that, then you have the wrong director. I thought Odets ruined a very nice show he wrote, called *The Flowering Peach.*

QUESTION: What could he have done with it?

MR. KAZAN: It could have been a beautiful play. First, a director would have said to him, "Rewrite!" He would have straightened the script out. No author's going to do that alone. Once an author puts himself in a position where he's proof against criticism, it's awful. Tennessee always says, "Lift your voice! Lift your voice! Give me more melody in your voice! [Laugher.] I don't get enough lilt out of your voice!" That drives the actor nuts! [Laughter.] Other authors just sit there and check each word. [Laughter.]

QUESTION: I feel that a great deal of the so-called writing of the play takes place right up there on the stage. For myself, I felt I'd gone about as far as I could go with words on a paper. Then in rehearsal I did cuts and so forth. But I think a playwright should get one good chance to direct his own play.

MR. KAZAN: Conflict, by the way, is very creative. Within limits, of course. You asked me about producers, and this is going to seem terribly arrogant and shameful, but I don't like any of them! No, I really believe there's a fine, valid relationship bond between an author and a producer-director. The job of the director is to bring to life the author's work, and he has to do it through scenery. That shouldn't be left to a producer. Costumes, lighting effects, music, casting—all of that is creative work that has to be done through that bond. Personally, I don't like another person in it. Although the producer's necessary for business, and I appreciate it when he's good at business.

QUESTION: Do you think the theater's in a healthy state today?

MR. KAZAN: There are healthy elements in it now. Off-Broadway is a healthy thing. It provides channels of production where things can be seen. I think there are more good young actors now, due largely to the work that was started in the Group Theatre and has kept going through all these organizations. I find more good young actors. The mid-'40s, when Williams and Miller and Inge and those fellows emerged, was a more exciting time. But whether they were individual phenomena who came out then and made those times seem better, I don't know.

QUESTION: Do you think the theater is verging on a freer form of staging?

MR. KAZAN: Yes, I really do. I know I'm interested in it. Some playwrights seem to be tending that way. One thing that stops it is the kind of theaters that we have. They're all built on the old model. I mean we're aiming at a freer stage platform—a theater as more of a platform in the middle of an audience with nonrealistic effects, rather than a box that you look through into a lantern slide.

Among the scripts I've read, there have been several in which people talk directly to the audience. That was started in *Cat on a Hot Tin Roof.* Not really started, but first used in recent history. Saroyan had it too. And Thornton Wilder did it before that. There is a tradition for it. *Strange Interlude.* O'Neill did that himself. No director did that.

QUESTION: *The Great God Brown* and even Shakespeare.

MR. KAZAN: Shakespeare was a director as well as a playwright. Probably he was a producer too, artistically.

QUESTION: Why break the relationship between the audience and the stage? Why can't you put what they're saying to the audience in action?

MR. KAZAN: The direct approach is more effective.

QUESTION: You do it just for the sake of the effect?

MR. KAZAN: It has a tremendous power in its directness and its candor. If the whole thing is done in that style, I think you can have a tremendous effect. You have it in all kinds of presentational theater. Songs are sung right at the audience. It's as though you're saying, "I'm not bluffing here. I'm telling you and it goes like this . . . ," then you go into the action. It has a great direction and strength.

QUESTION: What do you think about Brecht's whole idea—the relation with the audience?

MR. KAZAN: I like it a lot. They're sitting out there and you're conveying to them by all the means you have the thing you want them to experience.

QUESTION: This is the theater . . .

MR. KAZAN: Yes, this is the theater and there's no bluff about it. Brecht got it, I think, from the Japanese theater. In the Japanese theater often a character comes out and introduces himself. He does a half-dance, half-song which presents his viewpoint, his mission, and what he's searching for. There's a tradition there and in this form it's possible.

QUESTION: But there's this so-called rule in playwriting that refutes your actor saying who he is and what his purpose is; that should be right in the action.

MR. KAZAN: The other technique was effective in *Waiting for Lefty*. That was a notable example of it.

QUESTION: They criticized it in Miller's *A View from the Bridge*.

MR. KAZAN: I didn't like the way it was done in *A View from the Bridge* either. Way on the side of the stage, they had a guy who was a lawyer and he was narrating it. It wasn't direct. It was as if they were sneaking it in, like the guy in the old reviews of the '30s who sang "A Pretty Girl Is Like a Melody." This guy talked to you and then he watched the action a bit. There was something artificial in that arrangement. If he'd frankly spoken to the audience more plainly and unashamedly it might have worked.

In the production of *The Princess Turandot*, the actors came out in their street clothes—bits of cloth and masks, etcetera—and lined up across the stage, bowed to the audience, presented themselves in their everyday clothes. Then they put on makeup right there in front of the audience. It was done like a series of planned movements. Gradually you watched the contemporary people turn into these fanciful figures from the past. It gave you the feeling that it wasn't the re-creation of that period, but a comment on that time.

QUESTION: Why do the directors working in moving pictures seem to be more imaginative in seeking out means of communication than they do when they're working on a play?

MR. KAZAN: In the movies, you have wind, animals, houses, weather; you have changing sky, mud, real food. You're not only photographing actors, but all the phenomena of life. What you say about the stage is true. Generally, you're expressing things through an actor who's experiencing and saying words that the author's written. In that sense it does seem confined. But when you get a play like *Death of a Salesman*, which opens up an inner world that no one has imagined before, the potential of the theater seems enormous.

QUESTION: Then why the insistence on naturalism in the theater, which doesn't lend itself to naturalism?

MR. KAZAN: I agree with you. I would shy away from it. In the theater the imagination is unbounded by realistic things. Nothing can do it except the theater.

QUESTION: You've said that the theater expresses the playwright and the film expresses itself.

MR. KAZAN: I don't exactly mean that, but certain elements are more at your command in the movies. In the movies, you get up in the morning and the first thing you do is look at the weather, which is a reality to you. Whether it's going to rain or snow, or the breath is going to show— all these things are the materials of art, really. And they don't exist in the theater. In *Grapes of Wrath*, if Steinbeck is describing a country scene, the things he talks about exist for you in the movies, but they don't in the theater. In the theater, some guy says, "It's sure hot today," and some Actors Studio actor takes out a handkerchief and does a heat exercise. [Laughter.] It's not the same thing.

QUESTION: Why can't the verse form or higher prose be applied to our average topic of today? Say, *Tunnel of Love?*

MR. KAZAN: No damn reason—it'd be a lot better. [Laughter.] Molière does it.

QUESTION: I mean as a convention of the modern theater.

MR. KAZAN: To hell with convention. As I say, John [McLiam], if you can do it, it would be wonderful. I think an attempt to try it in a comic form would be marvelous. I thought there was a lot of funny stuff in your play *[Sin of Pat Muldoon]*—an elaboration of what man might say directly. The Irish—I guess the Irish was a way of unlocking that, wasn't it? It made it seem real to you and the audience that a man could carry on entertainingly. He had some wonderful speeches, I thought.

QUESTION: Arthur Miller was here and he spoke of kinds of theater: poetic theater, heroic theater, etcetera. He felt that after one is able to do the craft of theater in terms of writing scenes that will make people laugh or make people cry, a playwright gets bored with this and tries to go into something else, something beyond craft. Do you as a director, having developed great skill over the years, have a point of view similar to Miller's?

MR. KAZAN: Frankly, about one-half of the time I get disgusted as I repeat myself. You've done scenes in that particular way before, and methods and solutions often rush to your mind and you often, too late, realize that they are memories and former solutions. You do have a sense that you're in danger of becoming facile.

QUESTION: It seems to me from Miller's talk that he wanted to get rid of the effect that would evoke emotion. Do you agree with this?

MR. KAZAN: I don't know what it means. Explain it to me.

QUESTION: Well, in his terms, in writing a scene that would shock someone, say, sexually—or shock in terms of violence or evoke a big yuk . . .

MR. KAZAN: He wanted to get rid of that?

QUESTION: Well, I think he wanted to go beyond that . . .

MR. KAZAN: Then why did he have one man kissing another in *Bridge*?

QUESTION: Brecht puts the theater on a didactic level. He has something to preach. He gets you into emotion and then cuts it off completely, so that you're more aware of being in the theater and more aware of what he wants to say.

MR. KAZAN: He says something about direct connection with the audience and using a frank presentational quality. That's healthy and can be very exciting theatrically and very useful in the projection of certain themes. If you're adapting novels, I think that technique can be terribly useful. Or if you are dramatizing a legend, or something where dance is important, or where extra-mental or extra-rational means are employed, it leaves you free to use more means than just those of speech and direct dramatic scene.

QUESTION: Getting back to Arthur Miller, I think he meant more of a lecture than emotional-type theater. He brought up the fact that in our theater today none of our heroes are very intelligent. He said he was trying to write a play where the man was intelligent and aware, and that he was no longer interested in an emotional character. He felt the problem should be more articulated rather than just being expressed in terms of experience. Yes, a character should be fully aware . . .

MR. KAZAN: Of his own disaster? Yes, I think there is a point there. Except I just object to the exclusivity of any statement like that. Why be exclusive about it? I think it all depends on what you're trying to say in a particular piece. I do think that if a man's aware of his own tragedy it can be a source of great emotion, of great poignancy or meaning.

QUESTION: Mr. Kazan, will you express yourself on the question of "taste" in the theater?

MR. KAZAN: Well, I didn't see *Ten Commandments*. [Laughter.] But I've been guilty of bad taste sometimes. I've been excessive or gone past the bonds of truth, or let the effectiveness of the scene carry me past what it really would be in life. I would say that if you're untruthful, or just theatrical for its own sake, you can be in bad taste. You're prostituting.

QUESTION: Do these things that come out in your talks with a playwright prior to rehearsal include the extent to which you take a scene?

MR. KAZAN: Yes, you should, but those things aren't usually talked about. There's a little rule that I have that may be of use: How far you go with a scene is in the department of style, and if you look and examine a playwright closely, you can get your sense of style from him. For example, if you know Sam Behrman [playwright S. N. Behrman], you know he's what he is; his plays should be done in the Behrman style and the actors chosen should be Sam Behrman actors.

In other words, the actors should have wit, sensibility, deftness, ability to speak lines lightly and with an understanding of their point, a sympathetic emotionalism without anything turgid, and so on. You see, in describing Behrman, you find the style—the dimensions or the boundaries, so to speak—within which you should operate.

The first job I give myself is to get to know the playwright, to know what he or she is like, so that I'm operating within the bounds of the individual personality. I try to express the playwright and his material, rather than my own material.

QUESTION: But how can the playwright help communicate these things to a director other than just saying, "Understand me"?

MR. KAZAN: Eat together, go out for walks together, talk, get to know each other. Get him to know you outside of your play. There are actors who're good for Williams. They have his particular quality in them. And Miller has his own quality. You have to find his style and implement it with the material to fit that style.

QUESTION: Will you say a little about what your own attitude is on what essentially makes a good piece of dramatic writing?

MR. KAZAN: It's good if it illuminates something in the audience's own experience, helps them to see more, know more about themselves, know more about the lives they live. If it's something to illuminate or kindle. I think that's the greatest thing that can happen. Somehow something is opened up or revealed for an audience.

QUESTION: Then a very simple, naturalistic play like Robert Anderson's *Tea and Sympathy* can, by these terms, be a great play?

MR. KAZAN: It probably could have gone deeper, or illuminated more deeply into their lives, been something more fundamental or more shaking. I thought *Death of a Salesman* did that more than any play I ever saw. It shook people. It shook me. It made me feel, "There's my father and there's what my relationship with him was." Something fundamental in my own life was revealed to me, and in a way relived.

QUESTION: Would you compare that play with *All My Sons?*

MR. KAZAN: I think *Salesman* was written more instinctively and less mechanically, more directly and more out of Miller's own experience. He wrote it in six weeks. He'd thought about it a long time, but it just flowed out in the writing. The form of it was not calculated. *All My Sons* was a piece that was constructed. The construction in *Salesman* came more deeply from the material and more organically from his relation to the material. I think perhaps that's the best American play of recent years. The scenery wasn't imposed on Miller. Jo Mielziner and I thought it up one day, and he liked it. He changed the play somewhat to fit our scheme.

QUESTION: How much of the original script resembled what we ultimately saw?

MR. KAZAN: I'd say very much of it. *All My Sons* was rewritten quite a bit before rehearsal under my influence, so to say.

QUESTION: I've found from my own experience that having merely a general idea of where the play is going is enough. How much in direction can a story like *All My Sons*, which was rewritten, be finally centralized and be made into a balanced piece?

MR. KAZAN: That's a fundamental craft problem that no one has solved—there's no solution. Everybody's struggling with that. There's form on the one hand and content on the other, and very often one does violation to the other. Or, if your considerations of form are too strict, you very often find yourself pressing or distorting without knowing it. On the other hand, if you don't have form, you're not working in the theater exactly.

QUESTION: I find myself imposing form sometimes, instead of letting form grow.

MR. KAZAN: I think experience and increasing skill will get you more where you'll construct without thinking about it. By the way, one of the things that made *Death of a Salesman* was that Arthur Miller had an extremely vivid image or memory of an uncle of his. In his knowledge of the uncle was the combination of a sense of the man's tragedy and a delight at the man's simplicity, the charm of his foolishness and the tragedy of his false ideals. In other words, the peculiar sense of values that is in *Death of a Salesman* was wrapped up in this one person, this uncle.

So he didn't have to say to himself, "I'm going to keep it balanced formalistically between a tragedy and a satire." Is that clear? It is to me, because Miller knew his uncle so well that he brought the uncle's unique personality to the play. I thought the movie was miserable. The director let the actors run away from him and they were self-pitying and breast-beating and the humor was lacking.

QUESTION: There was a lot of honesty in the play, but it was a superficial honesty that had a kind of banal quality to it. It was as though a lot of traveling salesman jokes were told with a catch in the throat.

MR. KAZAN: No, I don't agree.

CHORUS: No, no, no, no. [Laughter.]

QUESTION: There's a fine line between reality and this foolishness or absurdity of the businessman. The first time I saw the play I had this tremendous experience with [Lee J.] Cobb as Willy. Then I saw Thomas Mitchell play it, and the only feeling I got out of it was that Willy was some sort of fool. Mitchell pushed the absurdity or the comedy of it and it lost all its value. It's so delicately balanced . . .

MR. KAZAN: As a matter of fact, Cobb got unbalanced too. He was the best in the first two or three months, and then he went over in the direction of more self-pity.

QUESTION: Isn't that an example of how a play's values can be distorted by the work of the actor? The actor about-faces what is supposedly something genuine with tragic-comic aspects; suddenly all the values are lost because the actor approaches it in a certain way.

MR. KAZAN: Not all the values, but there was a change in effect there. When Cobb got self-pitying, the effect was something different from what Miller intended. You see, Miller intended that the man have, despite his tragedy, tremendous vitality and love for life, and although foolishly aimed, a great appetite for his goals. It was the peculiar combination of it that gave it something unique.

QUESTION: What would you say the central theme of the play is?

MR. KAZAN: I'm not much on that sort of discussion.

QUESTION: *Member of the Wedding* [by Carson McCullers] was a play that seemed to me so wonderfully done that everybody forgot there wasn't a very significant point to the play. But there were places where the excellent direction made the play go over. It can happen the other way: A good play gets such bad handling that the point never gets over.

MR. KAZAN: I enjoyed the play. I thought it was beautifully done and I thought it was beautifully directed. One of [Harold] Clurman's best jobs.

QUESTION: But do you think it's a good play?

MR. KAZAN: I thought it was a fine theater piece.

QUESTION: Did you really?

MR. KAZAN: I didn't think it was a very well-constructed play, but I enjoyed it.

QUESTION: It didn't answer what you said before . . .

MR. KAZAN: Oh, yes it did! I still remember that phrase "member of the wedding." My little girl nine years old just wants to be a member of every wedding. It does illuminate something—about a little girl's desire to get into life further—the mystery and enchantment of it for her. It did for me.

QUESTION: After you've gone over your script with a very wise director and you've hacked away and hacked away, don't you think that in the production something may be lost? Don't you think that's true of *Member of the Wedding*? Isn't it better sometimes for the director *not* to help the playwright?

MR. KAZAN: It depends on the play, really. O'Neill wouldn't let you. You couldn't have any conversation with him. He knew exactly what he wanted to say. I do think *Member of the Wedding* is redundant. It's a wonderful play, but on the other hand, I think it could have been more moving, maybe. But with O'Neill, you could never have any conversation with him about cutting his play. I once had a talk with him, and he was a man that you felt was writing his destiny. Also, he was a man really brought up in the theater. I think that man was trying to put down every goddamned thing he felt about his youth.

You say some authors write about themselves. I think [Thornton] Wilder did. That happened with *The Skin of Our Teeth*. I recognized it. I didn't ask for any rewriting on it. I thought it was wonderful. There was no rewriting except a tiny bit on the beggars. Wilder extended them a little bit. He wrote about a page and a half; no other rewriting was done. He had a right to ask that it be done his way, and I did it.

QUESTION: The identity that's created between an audience and a play—the stronger it is, perhaps the greater the play. Now, sometimes you write a play in which you're trying to break out of a formal convention and you begin to use techniques which aren't too well known. These techniques, once used, break the empathy of the audience and the play.

Take *Camino Real*. I could understand why some people couldn't identify with it because of all this new stuff around them. So, when a playwright wants to take flight, he's faced with something that he can't help: that the audience is just not used to these new forms. The identity of the audience to the play is lessened. In a sense, is it the education of the audience to these forms?

MR. KAZAN: Well, you're a man and the symbols that can be meaningful to you can be meaningful to other people.

QUESTION: Would you take a chance on another *Camino Real*?

MR. KAZAN: Sure. Right away! I'd do it better, too.

QUESTION: Over the period of the rehearsals, you and the author guide the actors in the direction you want. You open. And after months of playing, as you said happened to *Death of a Salesman*, the actors drift away from the pattern that's been established. Do you have any way to bring them back?

MR. KAZAN: There's no damn way they can ever come back. You can rehearse and rehearse and rehearse, but the thing that exists in the performance when it's right is made up of interlocking relationships. The actors have it before they open, and before the critics and the wives have spoken. You do your best. You have rehearsals and you bring it back and you talk. Some shows I've kept up, and some I haven't tried to keep up. I would say that since it's an organic thing, you never really get it quite back to where you think it should be.

The point is, you try. Sometimes it's easier than others. In *Tea and Sympathy*, where the problems of the actors were simpler, it was easier to keep in good shape. Deborah Kerr was very, very conscientious, and since she was the center of it and had a good relationship with the other actors and they with her, it kept together very well. In *Death of a Salesman* there was some trouble backstage. And it did deteriorate. Cobb left it after eight months. It was a blow the play never got over.

QUESTION: In directing a play, do you sometimes create a moment or crisis where the playwright may not have intended it? For the reason that you think it needs it?

MR. KAZAN: Yes, I'm guilty of that. And it's been abundantly pointed out to me that I sometimes do it where it shouldn't be, or that I overstress. I think that criticism of me is correct. Sometimes you do it legitimately. Sometimes you put in a situation that's under a scene, that's not there.

Do you want to hear an old story? George M. Cohan was doing a play and he had a helluva good first act, and a second act that was good halfway through. At the end of the second act, there was a long scene between two characters in an office that went absolutely flat. They rehearsed it and they rehearsed it and they opened on the road, and the end of the second act was still going flat. So finally one day Cohan called a rehearsal of this other actor and himself and he said, "When my secretary announces you I'm going to say, 'Just a minute. Show him in in a minute,'" and he reached down and opened a desk drawer and removed a pistol; he put it on the table and covered it with his hand like this and said, "Now, show him in." [Laughter.]

That's the kind of thing you're talking about. A crude example, but you sometimes do that. Sometimes you whip up a scene by overlapping lines and stuff like that when it's dull. Directors do all kinds of things. Truthfully, what you should do is solve the thing that's wrong and not cover it up.

QUESTION: When you do this—hype a scene—is it after you've talked to the playwright?

MR. KAZAN: No, ma'am. It should be, but often it isn't. Maybe it's just instinctive with me. If I feel a scene just lays there, I do something. I did it a lot in the first act of *Cat on a Hot Tin Roof.*

QUESTION: It needed it!

MR. KAZAN: Well, you know, I was oppressed by the fact that that girl was jawing at that fellow for fifty-two minutes, or whatever it was. And I did do things. For instance, I had certain scenes where they said, "Shh, no one must hear." You know, that's an old director's trick.

QUESTION: In the choice of a director and whether he's famous . . .

MR. KAZAN: Find out what he's like as a human. It's much more than his damn technique or his bloody credits. Know him, find out if you can get close to him. See if his experience is related to yours.

QUESTION: It seems to me that in the last ten years it's been the director who's seized control. It's been called a "director's theater" and . . .

MR. KAZAN: Well, speaking against my own kind, the director should really be working for the author, conscientiously trying to put that author on the stage. The director's the executive. But essentially, he's obligated to realize the author. There may be the "power play"—it exists more in musicals. A musical can be chaos. You really do have warring elements. For example, a songwriter is a songwriter, no matter what he says and no matter how artistic he is, no matter if he quotes Brecht and every other goddamned thing in the world. [Laughter.] He wants his man to get out there and belt the song stage center. He wants it there and he wants everyone else to shut up!

But the book writer is trying to keep the integrity of his story going. The director is in there between these two, and the dance director says, "I'm not getting enough rehearsal time. [Laughter.] I can stage that song better and get some life in that song." And now, choreographers are staging songs and the songwriter naturally thinks they think his song is weak, so they are covering it with movement. [Laughter.] The scrap starts the first day—for rehearsal time and rehearsal space. I know, I've done three.

QUESTION: This communication between the director and the author as human beings; do you feel that groups such as the Group Theatre and the Moscow Art Theater, in which the playwright practically lived with the group, embody the atmosphere in which a playwright will most likely blossom?

MR. KAZAN: No, I'm leery of generalizations, "most likely" and all that. But that atmosphere is a good one for playwriting. Odets did get a helluva lot out of his life as an actor and his knowledge of actors in the Group Theatre.

QUESTION: When you started the Actors Studio, were you envisioning something in terms of an actors-directors-playwrights community group?

MR. KAZAN: Yes. I had that vision in my mind, but I've not been able to achieve it. It hasn't worked out. I think Lee Strasberg has made a contribution over there. There's a large body of actors that are trained together and they do have respect for each other and themselves and their craft. Most of them are much better off for their training; we've accomplished that much.

QUESTION: Mr. Kazan, wouldn't you say that one of the ways to bridge this chasm that exists between the playwright and the director is some sort of mixture, some getting them together to know each other?

MR. KAZAN: No one's been able to find out how to organize that. Playwrights are often isolated from practical work in the theater. Your group has made some efforts to solve this by having observers. I know I've had at least two or three on some shows.

QUESTION: Have you ever worked on a play before rehearsals and then when the actors came in gone back to the original version?

MR. KAZAN: Yes, I once did a disastrous thing like that. I did a play called *Jacobowsky and the Colonel*. On the eighth day of rehearsal I found I'd misdirected it and threw the whole damn thing out and started over again. I once worked all summer on a thing by Sam Behrman called *Dunnigan's Daughter*. I worked carefully and conscientiously, driving thirty miles a day, guiding him, being brilliant in conversation. [Laughter.] Being influential, and finally getting a script that was a disaster in the theater. Yes, everybody has done that!

I thought *All My Sons* was helped a lot by the rewrite work. I'm leery of last-minute rewrites. I do think you can get into an awful mess. I mean on the road. I've never had too much success with that.

QUESTION: Did you try Tennessee Williams' own third act of *Cat on a Hot Tin Roof,* or was that settled before you went into rehearsal?

MR. KAZAN: I thought it was settled.

QUESTION: But he didn't, is that it?

MR. KAZAN: In utter candor, I think he thought better of it later. I rather regretted several things he said in the preface [to the published edition of the play]. He had his right to have me choose to do it as he chose and I repeatedly said to him, "I'll do anything you want, but here's what I think. . . ." About ten days before we opened in New York, I said, "If you really think the other one's better we'll put it in." I also offered to do the other one in the road company.

QUESTION: From the preface I got the impression he thought you'd imposed that version on him for commercial reasons. In fact, I got the impression that you said, "Take it or leave it!" Since he would not leave it, he took it.

MR. KAZAN: I got that impression, too, and I didn't care for it.

QUESTION: Actually, what you're saying is, you offered to do his version.

MR. KAZAN: No, it was much more than that. We did discuss it very carefully. I did tell him what I thought. He talks about powerful directors; well, he's a very powerful boy himself. We did discuss it at great length. I really think his reversal was an afterthought. After the play had opened and it was successful, he thought, "My God, the other one is truer to what I was trying to say." He was not pressing me, either on the road or anywhere else, about the original third act. It was rather a shock to me when I saw it labeled "the Broadway third act" and the "original third act." There's some difference, but not a vast difference.

QUESTION: Didn't he sort of retract that in an interview with Mike Wallace on *Night Beat* recently?

MR. KAZAN: I didn't hear the interview. Did he?

QUESTION: Yes, he said some wonderful things about you. [Laughter.]

MR. KAZAN: Right now, I feel I wish I'd done his original third act if it meant that much to him, and if he does feel it's better. I don't want that on my conscience.

QUESTION: No, he said you didn't impose it on him . . .

MR. KAZAN: Well, that's right!

MR. HAMLIN: Thank you very, very much. [Applause.]

Paddy Chayefsky
(1923–1981)

Rewriting is a dilemma faced by every playwright. Paddy used to delight in relating this experience as symbolic of those frustrations.

Early in his career, Paddy had written a full-length play called *The Fifth from Garibaldi* (never produced), which had evoked the serious interest of a well-known, much respected Broadway director. Paddy and the director had discussed the play in detail and both agreed that it had problems that should be addressed. Paddy set about rewriting. When he had finished, they again discussed *Garibaldi*. The director felt that although progress had been made, additional work was still needed. Shortly thereafter Chayefsky submitted a third draft, and subsequently a fourth, a fifth, and even a sixth.

When the director still had reservations, Paddy went away. After a few weeks he returned with freshly typed pages, in a spanking new binder. The director read the play immediately and with great enthusiasm said to Paddy, "Now we're getting somewhere!"

The seventh version was the original manuscript.

Paddy Chayefsky was a native New Yorker and attended DeWitt Clinton High School and the College of the City of New York. He returned from army service in World War II, with a Purple Heart, to work briefly at an uncle's print shop before devoting himself to writing.

Paddy was one of the original group of the 1949 New Dramatists. He always regarded himself as a man of the theater, although his reputation was made in television. Among his most memorable TV plays were *Marty* (1953), which was made into an Academy Award–winning film in 1955; *The Bachelor Party* (1953), filmed in 1957; *Middle of the Night* (1954), filmed in 1959; and *The Catered Affair* (1955).

Other motion pictures Chayefsky wrote were *The Goddess* (1958); *The Americanization of Emily*, with Julie Andrews and James Garner (1964); *The Hospital* (1971), which won the Academy Award; and *Network* (1976), with an Academy Award–winning performance by Peter Finch.

For the stage he wrote *Middle of the Night* (1956), which starred Edward G. Robinson; *The Tenth Man* (1959); *Gideon* (1961); *The Passion of Josef D.* (1964), which he also directed; and *The Latent Heterosexual*, staged in London in 1968.

A New Dramatists Craft Discussion

with Paddy Chayefsky
April 16, 1956

Howard Lindsay introduces Mr. Chayefsky.

MR. LINDSAY: The New Dramatists have come tonight, for me, full circle. The first year it was formed we used to meet in a room up in the apartments over the Hudson Theatre. We sat around this table and talked, and there was a certain relaxed atmosphere. In the group, not always at the table—but far back in the corner—was Mr. Paddy Chayefsky. Occasionally this quiet person would ask a question. It was gratifying that he came into the theater with a play which I enjoyed enormously, *Middle of the Night.*

I've heard that those who saw the run-through before it left town were shattered by it. People have told me they couldn't talk for an hour after they left the theater. Then I heard about people who went to Wilmington and came back and said that this was one of the great plays of all time. Whatever Mr. Chayefsky tells you tonight about his mistakes, you'll say to yourself you won't make them. But you will. We learn what not to do, which is sometimes more valuable than what to do. I'm going to turn it over to Mr. Chayefsky.

MR. CHAYEFSKY: Thank you. Howard, that run-through in New York that everybody raved about was not a particularly good show. Actually, the first run-through that we had for just a handful of people was much better. The play went downhill steadily. I'm sure I know where: It can be put in a phrase, "Let's wait till Wilmington!" which I encourage every writer in this room never to pay any attention to.

You come to your play's first reading, in which a bunch of actors read your lines. For the first time other people are listening to it and you're not covering up the weak spots as you do when you read through it quickly yourself. You get embarrassed and you squirm. I always put a little "x," meaning "cut here" or "Oh, my God! Something has to be done here." It's a terrible experience no matter what show I do—television, movies, or the one stage play I've had on. On television, when the reading is over, I sit down with the director and I say, "That was a good reading, but I think we're in trouble. I don't know what the hell direction that play is taking in the second act at all."

They say what they think—or, in television where I work, they leave it up to the writer. And I go home and I rewrite it. And I rewrite it during the first two or three days of the rehearsal. If a show is scheduled to air on Sunday, by Tuesday that script is as good as I can make it up to the point where the actors take over.

In the theater, it doesn't work that way. I'd go up to the director and say, "Josh [Logan], I don't like that love scene in the second act. I don't know what the husband is doing at all. What can we tell the actors? I don't understand it." And he'd say, "Let's see how it plays in Wilmington." It's a little comical. I remember the first day we ever talked together about this play. I said, "Josh, I must tell you something. I come to the theater and I take notes, but I do not work after six o'clock at night. I don't believe in staying up in hotel rooms all night long. I work better at nine in the morning."

Well, from the first day in Wilmington until several weeks after we opened in New York, I was writing at night in hotel rooms until six, seven o'clock in the morning. I might be a little naive but I still think it's a fatal mistake to work after six o'clock at night, except to go to the theater and take notes. It was frankly a very bitter and unrewarding experience for me, and particularly disillusioning in many ways because I've always thought of the theater as my home ground. I know I achieved a certain notoriety in TV and in the movies. But whenever I was asked, I always said I was a legitimate playwright. It was the one place where whatever you wanted to say you could say, and on a level of artistry and craft that I thought couldn't be achieved in any other media.

The play had some very good stuff in it, but it blundered and floundered and I made mistakes that I thought I would never make five years ago. I think it was out of a kind of terror. So I think the basic lesson I learned was to depend on myself, even if I'm new at it.

MR. LINDSAY: Paddy, I hear you cut out a lot of laughs in Philadelphia because you wanted to be considered a more serious playwright.

MR. CHAYEFSKY: There's an element of truth in that. No laughs, though, were actually cut out. All I asked was that actors didn't play for them.

Josh is perhaps the greatest master of the broad, lusty comedy that I've ever seen. He took the first scene of act 2, Howard, which was badly written, disorganized, and very thin, story-wise, and he made it one of the most attractive scenes in the show by artful direction.

MR. LINDSAY: I'd like to bring up a question here which is at the heart of rehearsal. It's very difficult for the actor to get his direction from two different people. That is why the protocol should be that only one person, the director, should talk to the actors.

MR. CHAYEFSKY: Absolutely right.

MR. LINDSAY: Josh has been criticized by some authors for changing the script, for a dictatorial attitude.

MR. CHAYEFSKY: He didn't change a word. He never asked me to do a thing that I didn't do on my own. He broke his back. The play was never a very, very good play. It was at best a good solid production, and that's what came out, a good solid show. It had no extra style, no extra charm. There were holes in the script, and I'd rather talk about that.

Starting from the very beginning: The female lead was a difficult part to write. Yet she figures prominently in the opening scene. It's a very difficult scene to open the show, but as written originally it wasn't bad. It's what's called in the movies a "hook," a clever scene to catch your interest rather than a deep or insightful scene. It was supposed to be a girl who came home to her mother, to whom she could absolutely not relate at all, and to whom she had to pour out her heart. Out of this, we were supposed to find out not only that she was leaving her husband, but also what was wrong with the marriage.

But we never learn what was wrong with the marriage. That's my fault. I never sat down and said, "What the hell is wrong with that marriage?" until we hit Philadelphia, where the hole showed up at the second-act curtain. At that time, the stairway scene between the husband and the girl was the second-act curtain. I had to write a scene and the actors had to play a scene, and no one knew what the husband was to the wife or what the wife felt for the husband or why she married him in the first place. I finally had to invent a very radical sort of latent homosexuality—a kind of sadistic quality—in order to justify our second-act curtain, which is a rather screwy way of going about it.

If I had sat down at the time of the first reading when I knew it and said to myself, "Well, Paddy, if by the first-act curtain we don't know what's wrong with this marriage, we're in trouble. . . ," I should have gone home, worked on it, thought it out, and talked it over to find out what should be done.

I couldn't work out—to the level of depth I wanted—how to understand this marriage. I didn't try seriously to give the audience some insight into this marriage so that the girl would not be as unpleasant as she seemed in the first scene. Josh was faced with the problem of taking this highly unpleasant girl and making her palatable to an audience. Usually an audience wants to like the hero and the heroine. Well, nobody liked this girl. I did. I understood her. But I couldn't show the audience. This is nobody's fault but mine.

MR. LINDSAY: This girl was more the ordinary girl, the representative girl, but she didn't have a sensitiveness that her husband offended.

MR. CHAYEFSKY: Of course, I didn't want the husband to be a boor, or a monster, or a sadist. I wanted to tell the story of a girl who couldn't fit into a normal marriage. I wanted the husband to be a perfectly normal fellow who didn't know what the hell he did wrong.

MR. LINDSAY: I got that the thing that was wrong with the marriage was that the only time there was any connection between the girl and her husband was in sex.

MR. CHAYEFSKY: That part I meant to show. Actually, I wanted to say in the most sordid conceivable surroundings, the most ordinary and cheap affair, with the most recognizable people, that life can be beautiful, that there is fulfillment, that love is happiness. In other words, when people say this is a small play, my gorge rises. I thought I was talking about the deepest things of personal life. What is happiness and what isn't?

Well, I had to tell the story then of a man of fifty-three who fell in love with a girl of twenty-four and they get married. I would hardly think that this is what they call in analysis a healthy adjusted relationship. Certainly the fact that Eddie [Edward G.] Robinson plays this fellow as a charming and rocklike man is sheer nonsense. Any man who marries a twenty-four-year-old girl at his age has problems. I had to show two neurotic people.

Well, starting with the girl. She had to be neurotic. This is just working backwards.

How do you lay it out? Well, what kind of girl is she, then, if she's so neurotic? She has married. But she can't get along with the young fellows. There's something missing. She needs more than a normal young adjusted fellow can give her. The young guy can give her normal sex relations, an amiability, even kindness. She needs more. She needs an older man. What does she need an older man for? Well, probably in pursuit of some kind of a father which she never had. All right. Her father ran away when she was six. It always amused me, Howard, when I read that writers write a detailed biography of their characters. It sounds contrived.

In working backwards, I don't know the people until the demands of the script tell me what I have to put into a character. Well, I got a skimpy kind of a thing: A girl's father ran away. She never knew her father, couldn't get along with the young fellows—why, I never bothered to figure out, and I went to work on that. By the time I had spent almost three weeks on the first scene, I should have known. If I can't write the first scene in three weeks, there's something missing. I should have worked out what this girl really was. Here's my advice: If you're having trouble writing your first scene, *stop!* Sit down and figure what is missing in your own interpretation, find out why you can't find a legitimate honest line in the scene.

MR. LINDSAY: You started to talk about these two neurotic people, that you didn't know enough about the girl . . .

MR. CHAYEFSKY: The man I knew inside out. When I read a certain critic's column who said that Mr. Robinson lifts a rather small play to heights occasionally, I wonder who the hell would be bad in that part? It's a helluva good part—full-bodied, rich, complex, with perfect linear development. The girl, though, I couldn't get. And if you can't get your main character or your second lead, you run into so much trouble in your second and third acts. You have no resolution. There was nothing in the girl to resolve.

To discover what is wrong with this guy, I started with my third act. It's a good tip. I started with the ending. What is it driving at? What am I trying to say? What is the resolution? Knowing that, I try to work back now, establish my curtain so that it's not a third-act kind of thing. I must know in the second act what to write to make them reach the third-act scene. I didn't do it in *Middle of the Night*.

There's a much more basic problem to *Middle of the Night*. It's the girl's story, whereas I wrote it as the man's story. I wrote it for Eva Marie Saint, who couldn't do it. We got Edward G. Robinson and I thought I was being very clever by switching the third act over to the man. In Philadelphia and Wilmington for two acts we're following this girl right through the story, and then she disappears for half an hour and comes for five seconds right at the end of the play. This is another bad mistake.

MR. LINDSAY: The resolution—because it seemed to come out of nowhere except that the people had changed their minds.

MR. CHAYEFSKY: That's it! It never came out of the girl. For minimal characterization of this girl, one more quality had to be added, one more incidental story value, one more thing that would build up to the third-act resolution. He says she's a bright girl. We never see how bright she is, how sweet she is. We never get anything except a kind of a sketch.

QUESTION: Did you ever sit down and discuss this whole play before you even put the production together?

MR. CHAYEFSKY: *No.* I rarely sit down and discuss a play with a director unless the director comes to me and says, "I don't know what you want me to do with this scene." If I have trouble explaining it, then there's something wrong. Go home and rewrite it. It needs rethinking.

Josh and I each took a script, sat up in his apartment, and he read. I would say, "I'm a little bothered about that line, Josh." He'd say, "All right, why don't we cut it from here to here?" Then I'd say, "Okay," or, "Why don't we cut that line and leave this line?" Then he'd say, "How would you like that read?" I'd say, "Well, this is kind of the idea."

I can't play it for Josh. I can only tell him what I want to come out of it. And I must have said eight thousand times to Josh, "That third act when Eddie G. Robinson comes home is a death scene. It's right out of *Camille*. This is a man *not* dying slowly. This is the last throes of his death and he dies." It's not a man saying, "Y-e-s." He's not melancholy anymore. He is at his wit's emotional end and he's ready for a collapse.

He's a man accepting old age. These are dramatic images. In life people do collapse a little more slowly than that. We assume whatever went on offstage has brought him to this point.

MR. LINDSAY: Do you think if you had had bad notices in Wilmington and Philly it would have been a help?

MR. CHAYEFSKY: I think so, Howard. Thoughts about *Middle of the Night* were based on fantasy. In Philadelphia people were wandering around saying they'll forget *Death of a Salesman*. Really! If only we had a couple of lousy notices. In Wilmington we didn't get such good notices, but we should have been blasted in Philly.

Of course, that good run-through was just about the worst thing that could have happened to us, psychologically. It was bad for me. I didn't like the show. I didn't like the run-through. I stood backstage where I thought I wouldn't see anybody, but I didn't know people had to go backstage to get out and everybody kept passing me and saying, "My God! What a show!" You go away saying to yourself, "Not bad." You let it go. But you still say to yourself that scene's bad anyway, but you don't take it seriously. You don't do your work.

QUESTION: I saw the original *Middle of the Night* on television. There was one thing that made the husband very clear to me in the TV version. The girl wakes up in the middle of the night—the nightmare scene. He wakes up too and instead of comforting her . . .

MR. CHAYEFSKY: You're absolutely right. That's the one indispensable scene, which I tried to cover in the first scene of the third act but which in the run-through was the second-act curtain. I tried to get too much in one scene. It comes down to a very basic principle: You can write only one story in a play, any play. I wrote two. This is the girl's story. She is the one who goes through the whole experience and finds something of fulfillment. At the end, she's the one who learns; she's the one who says, "My story." I made it the man's story. I must have a scene with the girl and her husband—must—through which we can show the audience exactly and graphically, right in front of them, the discovery that this girl makes. Is that the obligatory scene?

MR. LINDSAY: Yes. It's certainly one of them.

QUESTION: Speaking of the TV show again, it was the economy of words that made it so good.

MR. CHAYEFSKY: Thank you. If by economy of words you mean cutting, I'm the best cutter in the United States. Believe me, cutting is more fun than writing. I think you can take the worst scene in the world, Howard, and if you cut it until you don't have one extra word in it, it will play. It will play on its basic emotion.

MR. LINDSAY: A play should be two hours long at most. If you can have it that length when you go in rehearsal, you're much better off. The earlier you can see a scene is wrong—you see a scene is weak—the earlier you can get that right, the better. Paddy is sitting here saying that this play isn't good enough. A lot of authors who talked to the New Dramatists—Anderson, Sherwood—said the same thing.

MR. CHAYEFSKY: Bob Anderson asked Maxwell Anderson to recite the list of successes he had written and he said, "Well, I can tell you my flops."

MR. LINDSAY: And boy, he went through a long list, didn't he!

MR. CHAYEFSKY: I wrote a book. By George, I wrote a book in which I said, "Know your big moment and work backwards." I'll be damned if I don't get into that problem with this play. I start off and I say, "Oh, I know kind of vaguely what that is." Then I can't write my second act, because I don't know where I'm going.

MR. LINDSAY: Most of the bad plays around town that have wonderful first acts and pretty good second acts and no third acts are because the playwright starts to write before he knows where he's going. Quite often, you know the destination not only of the play, but of a scene, and it's hard to get there. Sometimes it's very good to just say, this is what she says when the curtain comes down. Now he would have to say that ahead of this, and finally you get the flow of the scene that way. This is very valuable.

MR. CHAYEFSKY: It's the one lesson I learn every show, and I never learn it. I don't know what it is, I guess an impatience to plunge into the script.

QUESTION: We had Josh Logan up and he said the big thing is to keep the audience under your thumb all the time.

MR. CHAYEFSKY: Under your heel!

MR. LINDSAY: Oh, yes. It is not an easy business. Another thing that Paddy said that is terrifically important—to know the end of the journey before you start. You can quite often back into a scene. Do you have any plans on *The Catered Affair*?

MR. CHAYEFSKY: All I know is I sold it outright and the first script was sent to me. My wife was pregnant at the time and MGM called me and said, "We have a list of writers here and since you don't want to do the picture, who would you suggest?" They went down a long list and I said, "I don't know. I don't know." We got to Gore Vidal and after all these "I don't know's," I said, *"No."* Three days later they hired Gore Vidal!

MR. LINDSAY: Have you seen the picture?

MR. CHAYEFSKY: No, but I read the first draft. I dictated six pages, single-spaced, commenting on what was wrong with the script, and finally said it's all wrong; it's not the story, and then I washed my hands of the *Affair*. Well, they've been getting rave reviews. I thought it was a very bad idea to bring in a writer. I went out to Gore and we talked and I was shocked at how receptive he was. I'd throw out the window any writer who came in to tell me how to write. He just listened to me and took notes and seemed very pleased. All I can say is that this speaks very well for Gore Vidal, as I am *not* a very easy fellow to get along with.

Anyway, I sort of worked out a step-by-step outline with Gore. One of the characters in the play is a taxi driver, and his problem is that the money they're going to use on this wedding was the money he had been saving for his taxi. This is really an old familiar sort of problem that you throw into a play. The trick is to make it seem real. So it isn't just, "My God, you're taking the money out of my savings for my taxi, which is all I ever wanted out of life, a pair of brown and white shoes and a taxi." What happens now in this script is a very common failing in movie writing, and in playwriting too. The minute the character comes on, all he ever talks about is his taxi. He comes in and says, "Ohhh, I had a terrible time tonight. Wish I had my own cab."

You only need to say it once but say it at an important time. Why not save all that business of his little dream of a taxi for a beautiful little scene all for himself, instead of wrecking whatever scene you could get to by telling the joke long before you get to it.

If I can be pretentious enough to say, I learned some things about writing. One of them is, don't make your point over and over again when you can give the main character his good scene. Let him make the point there. You know, I've learned from things you've said, Howard.

MR. LINDSAY: Tell me what I said that you remember.

MR. CHAYEFSKY: All right. Josh and I got into a discussion and he told me the one he learned from you: The greatest rule for writing in the world is, "Where's the love story?" Every time you're in trouble, stop and say, "Where's the love story?" The love story may be a guy in love with a priest or a man in love with his son. It could be anything, but that's your basic story. If you have a love story, everybody's on your side.

Josh said something you might have said, "Where does the villain kick the dog?" When do we know who is the villain in this story? When does the guy come on and kick a dog? And people say, "Oh, he's the villain!" Sounds silly? Sounds trite? You don't know how useful this little gimmick is when you're stuck.

To get to one of yours, Howard. In the beginning of the second act, tell the audience all over again who they're for and who they're against. You don't know how sound this is. You get to the second act and you say to yourself, "I have to tell the audience who they're for and who they're against." Then you say to yourself, "Wait a minute. I haven't shown them yet. Where did the villain kick the dog?" Put in your scene to show who's the villain.

The most important one I remember, Howard, is, "Whereever your biggest laugh is, make it your second-act curtain." Sounds like a gag? It's the most workable axiom I've ever had in my life. What that means to me! Where's the high point of your story? If it's in any place but your second-act curtain or the beginning of your third act, there's something wrong with your structure.

Another one—not yours, Howard. Garson Kanin once told me he was following Somerset Maugham around in his garden, I suppose it was on the Riviera. I just can't picture Somerset Maugham anywhere but in a garden on the Riviera. He said, "Mr. Maugham, do you have any rules about cutting?" He thought awhile and said, "Yes. If you think of it, cut it." If you think of it, something's wrong that's bothering you. Cut it!

MR. LINDSAY: My story is about Sam Harris, one of the great producers in the theater but a very ill-educated, inarticulate man. He had been a prizefight manager, but he knew theater. He was about the first fellow to say, "Who am I rootin' for?" In this play I did with him back in '30, we had a villain in it, but Sam said, "Look, I don't hate him enough!" That is so basic. Josh says I helped him with *Mister Roberts* because when he read it to me, the thing that clarified their minds was when I said, "This is a love story between Mr. Roberts and the crew. Man meets crew, man loses crew, man gets crew."

MR. CHAYEFSKY: Here's some other ones you told me: "If you have a comedy, make sure all your curtains are laughs. If you have a drama, make sure all your curtains are serious."

"After you've asked all these questions and you're wondering what's holding up the show, cut out your side characters and give the lines to your main characters." Now that sounds awfully cursory and awfully abrupt but, by George, if you do you'll find that you really don't need that guy. It would be a better scene with the main character in it instead of the butler or the cousin.

MR. LINDSAY: That's one I don't remember saying.

MR. CHAYEFSKY: It amounts to this for me. I never had a character in a script who wasn't there because the story demanded it. If you write a character who has no plot value at all, cut him out.

I develop my characters according to the demands of the story. Otherwise, I find if I sit down to write about my mother I never get a story out of her. But if I sit down and say, "What does my mother mean? What is the story I want to tell about her?" How she went out to get a job. Then I say, "All right, forget my mother. This is the story about an old woman who goes out to try to get a job," and don't try to create my mother. Try to create the woman who's going to tell the story. Bob Anderson taught this. A great thing I always start off with on every script: Who wants what? What does the hero want?

My analyst doesn't pretend to know much about the theater, but he thinks that an audience likes to feel there's a strong person up there they can count on. It all comes to who are you rooting for in the end.

QUESTION: This business of working back, knowing the end of your play, do you feel there's a value in knowing the end of the individual scenes? When you start working on one act of a play, do you work back from the end of the act?

MR. CHAYEFSKY: Yes, I do. I sure do.

QUESTION: Do you work back from the end of a scene, the end of a peak?

MR. CHAYEFSKY: You don't have to . . .

MR. LINDSAY: If you have your play constructed, you know you're going to meet a certain situation, just as Paddy did here. You say, "I feel he has no right to marry this girl. It would be a big mistake. But he's made up his mind and something has to destroy that." Then you begin to figure how. All right, the reasons. The one who can do it best for him is his daughter. What kind of a girl is she? Then you go back and you prepare for it.

MR. CHAYEFSKY: This doesn't mean you go out and say, "What's my third act?" before you think of what you're going to write about. Actually, I suppose what happens to me and what happens to most writers, you get a feel. Something happens; something starts you off. It can be anything. I've always wanted to tell the story of my mother. Whatever you think the story of your mother is.

I sat down to write this story, and you can stumble and lurch and say, "Oh, that's a good first act. I'd love to write that scene." All of a sudden after you've mapped out two acts, kind of stumbling in painfully and smoking much too much, you suddenly figure, wait a minute, the third act has to be this. Then you start this reasoning, after you've worked for four months on the first two acts.

All that painful working out has to be reorganized again to lead up to it. This is what I call working back. I work back from my acts. But I don't think I work back inside the scenes. I know what the scene is going to say before I sit down to write it. I try to write it to the point of the scene. Usually, by the time I get to the middle of the first act, I know exactly where I'm heading in that act, so each scene builds toward that. I wish I could be that artful about the whole structure of the play. I'm very good at putting acts together, but not at putting the whole play together.

MR. LINDSAY: You don't do this while you're creating—while you're getting the idea, while you're thinking it up, while you're dreaming up the story. But after you think you've got the story and you have to organize it, to make sure it builds, that's where these things come in. "Have I got a beginning, a middle and an end?"

QUESTION: Take *Life with Father*. That had no villains, nobody kicking dogs.

MR. CHAYEFSKY: The basic story was the baptism.

MR. LINDSAY: Yes. I'm trying to phrase it. Father meets baptism. It's really Mother meets baptism, loses baptism, gets baptism. Father was the villain in *Life with Father*.

QUESTION: If he was the villain, but you were rooting for him.

MR. LINDSAY: Oh, you liked him . . .

MR. CHAYEFSKY: That's the use of the word "villain." Actually, the villain is anybody who gets in the way of the success of the hero.

MR. LINDSAY: In *Life with Father*, Father never won a battle. Mother won all the battles and the audience loved it. Well, for them to love it, she had to be the hero and he had to be the villain. He was so damn self-assured and laid down the rules and everything that the audience . . .

MR. CHAYEFSKY: Wanted him to be pinpricked.

MR. LINDSAY: He was just too damn difficult to live with. They wanted him to get his comeuppance. Technically, Father was the villain.

QUESTION: What do you do when you're writing a play and you have it all planned out, and you suddenly find one of the characters running away and you cannot stop him?

MR. CHAYEFSKY: If you find yourself writing a play and another character starts taking over, you really want to write about this other character. It's a pretty sure thing. You may have a much better play.

MR. LINDSAY: A character can run away with the play. Often it's the character who is the author. That's the character to watch out for, because they usually talk too much.

MR. CHAYEFSKY: I have a tendency to make people like this awfully wise and say all kinds of clever things. I have a rule. I always write all the wise and clever and philosophical things in, and then promptly cut them out. I leave some of them in because sometimes you simply have to lay it out.

One of the problems I had to beat is that I couldn't stand saying the flat fact of the scene. Somebody has got to say, "I love you." You think that's so flat. But somebody has to tell the audience that the guy loves the girl. You think, "My God, I can't lay it out like that!" You have to. In dealing with actors, you'll find they want to change all kinds of lines around. I let them have their head very frequently. I find there are maybe five or six lines in a script that are indispensable and cannot be touched. Those are the lines where you lay it out. If you don't say them, then the play doesn't make sense.

It's one of the problems Josh said he had with a lot of writers, and he had it with me, too. I kept saying, "Josh, you don't have to make it that thick or that bald. It's clumsy." But you'd be surprised how those clumsy lines play. They pack the biggest wallop. Cut out everything but a line that tells you what's going on.

MR. LINDSAY: That you have to have. Watch out, there's another character—sometimes it's this very character we're talking about now—one character in there who works for the author. I don't say there should be. I don't say that this is good. But there's one character who kicks the plot along. It's usually the least rewarding character that no actor wants to play, because they come in and say something and you can play the next scene. They're working for the author, but very seldom does the author work enough for them.

MR. CHAYEFSKY: I've heard one thousand times that Josh Logan wrecked the beautiful, artistic *Picnic*, that Bill Inge wrote. I know Bill. I've seen some of his plays. I cannot believe that Josh did anything but help that show. Bill is involved in the Chekhov mood; he wants all things to return to the circle at the end of the show. I don't know why everybody thinks Chekhov writes circles; he doesn't write circles at all for my dough.

And the kind of thing that Josh must have shoved in by brute force—let's face it, Bill Inge asks for this. Josh says, "Look, I don't care what we put in the third act, but if the audience doesn't go out saying 'hurrah,' there's something wrong with the play. She must marry that man. She must!"

Frankly, I tried to shove an ending on Josh, saying let's avoid the third-act ending. I guess what I'm really saying is, you've got to know your own play. Nobody can write your lines for you. Never let anybody do your thinking for you. Never write to satisfy anybody. Even if it's Gadge Kazan, Josh Logan, or Howard Lindsay. If it doesn't make sense to you, it's going to be lousy when you go home.

Just for the sake of confusion, I'll throw in one of Gadge's maxims. He once said to me, "Our kind of theater is the *progression of feeling*." That always makes me think of one thing you said, Howard: Is the play worth writing? Did you have something to write about? Was it worthwhile spending from three months to six months putting it together? In the end, was it worthwhile to have done it?

That scared me to death when I heard you say that, Howard, because I never knew. How could you tell if it was really worthwhile? Well, I got a pretty good criterion from Gadge's thing. If what you want to write is what stirs you emotionally, makes you either cry or feel good or whatever it is, and if you can convey this emotion to the audience, the play is worth writing. Well, to get to the rather diffuse part of Gadge's maxim, exactly what the hell does *progression of feeling* mean? I like to think that's my kind of writing. That is to say my plot, my elements of suspense. It's not a mechanical thing but I try to make it so. What I pick for my third act as an emotional moment.

In *Middle of the Night*, let me say again it should have been the girl's moment, but I made it the man's moment. It was his utter collapse in his acceptance of old age. This is a very dramatic moment and it should have come off like a million dollars. It didn't. When he put that shawl around his legs, you should have bawled your eyes out. Well, my plot was then based first, second, and third act up to this moment. How do I move this man emotionally up to such a point? This is the structure of a play. How do I make a man accept old age, a man who was fighting it?

Somebody said to me in Wilmington, "You know, if your man died at the end of the play, it would probably be a lot more successful." I said,

"You know, if I made this a tragedy and I said, 'Life isn't worth living and it's better to die and the industrial age is crushing us and what's the point of it all and the only good thing in life is a *Cat on a Hot Tin Roof*,' I might have had a masterpiece."

I like to say at the end of the show, "Life may be pretty miserable sometimes, but when you stop and look at it, it's worth living." Five years ago, I said to myself, "If I keep trying to be a genius, I'll never write anything." I pass this on to you. Don't try to make them masterpieces. Try to make them as good as you can and do each show as best you can.

A playwright once sent George Bernard Shaw a play. Shaw wrote back and said, "My dear sir: You are undoubtedly a genius, but unfortunately geniuses are a dime a dozen. What the theater needs right now is a playwright who knows his business and has been in his last position for several years." It's true. They say to a guy like Tennessee Williams, "Stop writing about those decayed Southern women!" As he once said, "It's like saying to van Gogh, 'Stop painting all those bright pictures!'" That's what he knows. That's what he writes better than anybody in the wide world.

MR. LINDSAY: You should be moved. But this will happen in a theater, I'll see a show and I know somebody in the cast, so I go back and tell them how much I liked the show and how good they were, and then I'll say, "And doesn't Esther give a wonderful performance?" And you get this raised eyebrow. But you mean it. And you say, "Doesn't she?" And the fellow says, "Well, look, if you'll think back, you'll realize the audience isn't supposed to like her. It hurts the play if the audience likes her. You liked her, didn't you?" "I loved her!" "You liked the character?" "Yes!" "Go back and look at the play again!"

MR. CHAYEFSKY: I'm afraid to go backstage.

MR. LINDSAY: We had a show out of town once and Moss Hart happened to be in the same city, and we asked him to look. After the audience got out, we sat down with him and said, "What do you think?" I've always loved his opening line. He said, "Boys, in New York you have to lie. But out of town, I don't think it's friendly." He told us what he thought was wrong. In town, we would expect "Saw your show. Great. Wonderful." But not out of town. It's not friendly.

I'd like to wind this up with a story about Josh that has nothing to do with playwriting but does have something to do with what we talked about tonight. He was out of town in Boston with some show, between acts in the lobby. There's a drunk who comes up to him and says, "Greatest goddamn director in America, you are. Greatest damn director." Josh says, "No, no, there are other very fine directors." The fellow says, "No. Greatest goddamn director." And Josh kept saying, "No, there are some other very fine directors." And this fellow said, "Name me another director as good as you are." And Josh said, "Kazan," and this fellow said, "You're right!"

MR. CHAYEFSKY: I hope the day never comes when I know how I write or why I write, because, to me, the minute you become that conscious of your own writing, there's trouble. You've lost your fun.

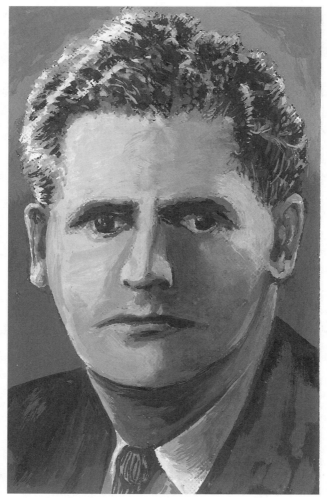

RENDERING BY JOSEPH LUBRANO.

Joseph Kramm

(1907–1991)

Time: A crisp autumn day in 1951. Place: Somewhere on 56th Street between 6th and 7th Avenues. Two old friends encounter one another:

"Oh, hello, Joe."

"Hello, Jo."

"How are you, Joe?"

"Okay, Jo. How's yourself?"

"Anything ever happen with your play?"

"So-and-so optioned it."

"And?"

"Nothing. Today the guy's option runs out."

"Joe, tomorrow send it over."

"Sure thing, Jo."

Three weeks later, Joe Kramm's first play, *The Shrike*, was in rehearsal and Jo *[José]* Ferrer was its producer, director, and star. *The Shrike* opened at the Court Theater on January 15, 1952. It won the Pulitzer Prize, the Donaldson Award, and the Newspaper Guild's Front Page Award.

Joseph Kramm's career in the theater began in 1928 as an actor with the Mae Desmond Stock Company in *Lilac Time*. He performed on

Broadway, toured on the road, and worked in London and with the WPA theater project in New York, during the Great Depression.

During World War II he served in the European theater of operations. By V-E Day he was a sergeant whose campaign ribbon bore five battle stars.

In addition to *The Shrike*, Kramm wrote *The Gypsies Wore High Hats*, which was performed at the Cape Playhouse on Cape Cod in 1952, on national tour with Kramm directing, and at the City Center in New York.

Build with One Hand followed in 1956. Its pre-Broadway engagement began in New Haven and came to an end in Baltimore. Also in 1956, *Giants and Sons of Giants* came to Broadway's Alvin Theater after a summer theater engagement.

A New Dramatists Craft Discussion

with Joseph Kramm
February 27, 1957

George Hamlin introduces Mr. Kramm.

MR. HAMLIN: Many of you were at the session held last week on the subject of rewrites. I believe Joe's going to have something to say about that tonight. Mr. Kramm.

MR. KRAMM: Thank you. I'm sorry I was late. I was rewriting. [Laughter.] I don't know what the tape is going to sound like—I'm chewing gum and I'm smoking.

I'm going to discuss the problems of rewriting from the viewpoint of the three areas of rewriting that Miriam [Balf] outlined to me. One, the problems of rewriting before anyone sees the play—that is, for the author himself. Two, the problems of rewriting when the play has been sold for production—that is, the problems involved with a producer and a director. And thirdly, the problems of rewriting after the play has gone into production.

Now, strictly speaking, there is so such thing as rewriting before anyone sees it. Someone must see the play before it is submitted to an agent or a producer. And I will stick with the agent because you will deal with an agent before you ever deal with a producer. If an author thinks he can write his play without discussing it or having it read by anyone, submit the play to an agent and hope that through his genius he has completed a work of art that will be accepted immediately, he is mistaken.

I have it on good authority that even Eugene O'Neill, who was more intransigent about his plays than an author has a right to be—even he discussed his plays with someone. And that good authority is Mrs. O'Neill. And she told me he discussed the plays during the writing and after the writing. The play was read by a friend.

An author sits himself in his room and writes. When he's finished he wants to know what he's got. Now here comes the first real problem in rewriting. What he's got—or what he thinks he's got—depends on several things. One, his own level of experience; two, his capacity for critical self-judgment; and three, his capacity and willingness to accept criticism from others. Now, this is extremely important. What point is there in learning a technique for rewriting if you are the kind of author who says, "No one understands me?" Or, "Idiots! What do they know?" You'll never in a million years be able to rewrite. Because you'll not be able to objectively evaluate what you've put on paper.

The problem of rewriting, then, becomes one of the personality of the writer as much as of the technique of rewriting. If you are the kind of person who has fallen in love with your words and you find yourself unable to submit your play to someone before it goes to an agent, you're going to discover problems in your work that you didn't know existed. And you'll discover that you'll become more and more unable to accept criticism. The ability to evaluate criticism from another is important. When you sit down to your problems of rewriting, maybe you dislike the person who gave the criticism. You aren't able to evaluate it properly. You don't know whether this is sound for the play. And the rewriting may suffer as a result. You may not like to hear it, but it's true. There are techniques which an author can use if he is objective enough to evaluate his work and accept criticism.

Of course, most authors *do* give the script to someone to read before they give it to an agent. You have to have another person's opinion because, inevitably, in working on a play, you do lose a kind of perspective. You find yourself too close to it and you're not able to evaluate it yourself. Now, if you don't want to discuss this play scene by scene or act by act with a friend, there is one very valuable thing an author can do. He can read it aloud to himself.

I don't care how badly you read. I don't care if you're the worst actor in the world, you should read the play aloud to yourself. Hear it with you own ears. You may discover that you are bored with certain sections of it. There's nothing like the actual hearing of the thing—because playwriting is *theater*. It is not in itself a literary form. And you mustn't think of it solely in terms of literature. The words have to be interpreted by actors and a director, and an audience must understand them.

Rehearsed readings and readings with friends are both valuable, but I can tell you from experience that you'll never really know what your play is like until you have it in front of a paying audience. Without that criterion, you'll never know. I don't bring any magic formula—I bring experience. I know there comes that stage in the writing when if you read it aloud to yourself, you'll find that you become aware of the discrepancies in your plot structure, in your character development, and actual lines you'll want to change—suddenly, as you say it aloud, it won't sound good to you. You'll discover that some of the characters sound very much alike, that you haven't given sufficient thought to the delineation of the characters in terms of the way they think and the way they speak. So, before you go for the objective opinion, if you'll read it aloud you will save yourself a lot of trouble.

Then comes the point when you give it to somebody to read. Now, this is where your ego is most likely to be offended. When people read the play, and they say, "Well, I don't know. It's a good idea. I think it needs this . . . or it needs that." Broad generalizations. The fact is, they don't want to hurt you. Don't submit your play to them, you'll learn nothing from it.

(You may think I lay a great deal of stress on the personal problems. I *do* because they're far more important than the techniques of rewriting.)

It's what you do about criticism and how you judge it. You give a play to someone to read, and if he's honest with you and says, "Well, if I saw this in the theater, I don't know if I'd like it," if your ego is offended, you're not going to be able to rewrite well. A successful rewrite is going to depend on your own personal capacity for self-criticism. No technique of playwriting is going to guide you. Only your own sense of what is right and wrong.

Many authors who don't have much experience feel that people are ready to tear their plays apart. They hug the play to their bosom and say, "No one must touch it!" They don't like the idea that they're going to have to work on it. Besides, finishing the first draft of a play takes so much out of you that when you finish you feel, "This is it!" It hurts to find that there is a great deal more to be done. But it has to be done, and you must accept that.

Now, when someone gives you criticism about plot structure or something in relation to character, if you accept it and know how to use it, you go back and you rewrite. If you're the kind of author who will accept a criticism just so far and no further, then you'll go back to your work, cross out three or four lines, substitute three or four different lines, and think that has solved the problem.

Most often, it does *not* solve the problem, because you haven't done any basic work. The person says to you, "I think this character should be more fully developed. I think that this aspect of the character needs to be brought out." Maybe a quality of selfishness, for example. So, you go back and you find a spot in the play and you put in a line or two about selfishness, and you think this answers the problem—but it doesn't. The idea of developing a facet of a character is something that's involved during the entire play. Again, this depends on your own ability to work, your laziness or your industry.

So, I come back always to *you* as a person—and *not* the techniques. You come to the point where someone suggests that the ending of the play doesn't seem to resolve the problems of the play. So you go to the play and you look at it and you look for the *easiest* possible way to find the answer. You change two lines at the ending, you bring your curtain down with a bang, and you say, "Ah, I've done it!" But you haven't done it at all. You'll find that the more you resort to the easy practice, the more difficult your rewriting will become!

For then you will lose whatever value you had in your original draft. You'll have a piece put in here and a piece put in there, and they'll stand out like sore thumbs. They'll stand out like they do in the scripts with the pieces of paper pasted in here and a few lines written in the margin. That's what your script will sound like. You must find within yourself the urge and industry to look over these things and say what is wrong with the play.

I want to skip a bit to get into the problems of a play in production, although the same things really hold true in any phase of the rewriting. I had a play tried out after *The Shrike* was written. It was called *The Gypsies Wore High Hats.* It was tried out in summer theater—it didn't come into town. I had my reasons for that—we couldn't cast it properly. But the story is this: *The Shrike* had been a success. So, when we opened on the Cape with *The Gypsies Wore High Hats,* all the Boston critics were there opening night. Why they came to an opening in stock, I'll never know! I spoke to them afterwards and they said, "Well, Joe Kramm's plays have to be reviewed—he had a success," and so on.

After the opening, everyone came to me—"Big success you're got! Another hit! You're in!" Gertrude Lawrence said, "You have a healthy baby." The next day the notices came out in Boston. They tore me to shreds. There was no play, they said. There was nothing, as far as they were concerned. The day that the notices appeared, everybody avoided me. They would see me coming and walk in opposite directions. The next day, Wednesday, one by one they got enough courage to come to me. "Joe, you know what I think is wrong with the play . . ." and they would start to tell me. Everybody told me what was wrong with the play. Members of the company, sixteen-year-old apprentices, the bartender, everybody told me what was wrong.

The point of this story is, I listened to everybody. I took notes on what everybody said—including the bartender and the apprentices. I did no rewriting that week. When I got all those notes together, I said to myself, "These people may not be able to discuss this in technical terms—they have a lot of suggestions about specific things that are wrong. But where they all hit on a particular point, I *know* something is wrong." I took those criticisms and went to work. We opened a week later. (We had a week off, so I had a week to rewrite.)

We opened in Dennis—the notices were very much better. Then I had a two-day layoff before we played the third week. I did more rewriting, based on these criticisms. The notices we got in Mountainhome were raves. And we would have done the play, but we couldn't cast it. But that isn't the point. I'm speaking about rewriting—and how able or willing you are to accept criticism and work with a viewpoint to helping your play. In the theater, the most honest opinion you can get is from the cleaning woman, or the stagehands. If they stop and listen, you know you've got something. If they're bored and continue their work, there's something wrong with your play.

You must not reject criticism because people may not know technically how to tell you what's wrong. You are dealing with human beings when you write a play. Get some people to listen to your play before you submit it to an agent. If you're observant and you discover when the legs begin crossing and the cigarettes begin lighting, you'll know what's wrong. You'll know *where* it's wrong—you may not know *what*.

Now, one frightfully difficult thing, and I'll be immodest enough to say that I do it, when I rewrite a scene I tear up the old scene. That's so I'll not be tempted to look at it again and salvage. The big problem of writers is that they're trying to salvage all the time. I made that mistake when I was working on *Build with One Hand*. I found myself lazy and did try to salvage, and the scene didn't go well at all. I was only able to work when I tore up the old thing and said, "If I'm not able to create this again, then there must be something wrong." Too often, when authors begin to rewrite, they salvage some precious line—they try to hold on to it in some way. And frequently, the precious line has nothing to do with the quality of the scene that the rewriting demands.

It's a lot better for your discipline if you tear up the old thing and start over. You will find that you'll not only be able to create again, but you'll be able to create with a fresher mind. You won't be holding on to old things—which, in their ways, are clichés.

Another problem is falling in love with a character. You discover the character doesn't really belong in the play, and you say, "I love this character. I love the things he says. I can't cut this character out." You must. No matter how precious these things become, you have to be ruthless. Amputate—cut!

Now, you get to the point of sending the play out. You've had friends read it and you've heard it read, and you decide after having done some work on it that you're ready to show it to an agent. Now, we sometimes wonder at the critical judgment of some of our agents, but good, bad, or indifferent, they do have an eye for the commercial.

If you bring anything to them that they can sell, they'll accept it. But then the agent will say, "I think you need to do more work on it." And you think you've done absolutely all the work that's necessary on the thing. But the agent thinks you've got to change the end, or the second-act curtain, or that you haven't really told your story.

Now to go into all the technical problems of whether you've told your story or not, whether your characters are three-dimensional characters—these aren't problems I can discuss in terms of rewriting. They're basic. If you haven't got real characters, then when you start to rewrite, your characters will remain cardboard.

I wrote eight plays before *The Shrike*. Someone said to me, "How did you have the courage to start the second one?" I wrote eight and none of them were ever done. I've written two since *The Shrike* and one of them wasn't done. The second, *Build with One Hand*, was done. The point is that to the extent that you learn and grow, to that extent your techniques improve. To that extent your ability to rewrite will improve. Because no one can change your own weaknesses, in terms of writing, for you.

All right, the agent accepts the play. The author is finally told that a producer likes it and wants to produce it. Glory be, the great day has arrived! The producer calls you in and says, "I like the play very much. I want to do it. I think if we get the right star for this, we'll have a hit. But I think you oughta do some work on the play." Now, each time you hear that, it becomes more and more discouraging, because each time you hear it you have thought that your work was finished.

Now, what you do about what the producer and director suggest comes back to the things I said before: To what extent are you able to evaluate their criticism? The producer will tell you things about the play that you've perhaps heard from other people, and they may be good ideas. As you listen to them again, if you are sufficiently flexible to accept new ideas, you'll be able to use them. Nearly all authors hear from fellow authors on Broadway: "Don't let them touch your play! They'll ruin it!" And it's often true. Maybe a play has been ruined by a producer or director's ideas. But only to the extent that you know what's valuable and what's not will you be able to rewrite the play.

Now the problems are different, because now you're working toward a production. Actors are going to come in and read the parts. And here you must rely, if you're inexperienced, on the judgment of other people. You just can't sit back and say, "This isn't right," and stick to a preconceived notion. Any person in the theater—I don't care if he's actor, director, or author—who thinks he is solely responsible for his work is out of his mind. Ideas come from everywhere and everybody. You simply can't say the other fellow doesn't know.

But the problems are more specific. From the producer's point of view, he's thinking of what it will look like when it's on the stage. The young author usually doesn't know what his play's going to look like on the stage. It has been said many times of authors that they may write well, but the stuff doesn't play. Only if the words fit into the mouth of actors and they come across as human beings will the play be successful. Now, this is where your own senses become sharpened, because now you're listening with a different ear. And you're reading with a different ear. You're listening to people whose experience, in terms of actual production, is far greater than yours. It would be wise to listen and evaluate these suggestions before you rewrite. The things they suggest are usually in essence the very things that were suggested to you before—things relating to plotline, structure, character development, ends of acts, and so on.

The problem of rewriting is heightened only to the extent that now it has to be faster. You don't have the time now to take the script home and say, "Well, maybe I'll do this and maybe I'll do that." If a production date is set, and the producers and director have talked to you, you now have to work with an acceleration that's going to provide results—because they're going to demand results. That day will come when rehearsals start, and you must have a script ready at that time. Your problems of rewriting will be helped or hindered, I assure you, not by techniques, but by your own growth in the theater. Once someone shuts you up in a hotel room and locks the door and says, "Rewrite the third act"—if you can't do it, you're lost.

In *The Shrike* we only had three weeks of rehearsal and one week out of town. But two scenes had to be rewritten in Philadelphia. I got up at six A.M., took three Dexedrine tablets, had a huge breakfast, and had the scene ready by noon. It went into rehearsal that afternoon and into dress rehearsal that night. I rewrote one scene on Friday and one scene on Sunday. Now I had two scenes to rewrite in the third act. The reason was that I had made Jim Downs' victory over the doctors and the people in the hospital and his wife much too easy. I didn't give him enough to overcome. You saw through it—you saw the device, the technique. So I had to rewrite.

The last scene of the second act was not too difficult for me to rewrite. But we opened on Monday in Philadephia, and Saturday night I asked a friend of mine, a clinical psychologist, to come down. I asked him several things in relation to some questions that are asked in the final ending, before the man is discharged. He told me. The next morning I went to work. I wrote the scene between six A.M. and noon. That afternoon it went into rehearsal and that evening it went into the preview, and Monday night we opened and there was no more rewriting.

Thank God. Except for one final thing—we cut out the final scene of the play. The scene wasn't necessary, so we cut it. We made that sharp cut at 12:30 in the morning and had no regrets about it. It's an example of another element of rewriting.

Now this is a problem: Your actors will be telling you what to say. There's a wonderful story (and I understand it's true) of a man meeting a star coming out of rehearsals, and the man said to the star, "Fine, we threw out the last of the author's lines today!" [Laughter.] This will happen unless you have the strength and ability to say, "This is what I think—this is what I believe," but you also must be able to evaluate what's good and use it.

Now, as far as New Dramatists is concerned, you have an enormous advantage here in being able to bring your play and discuss it with other people. But you also have a problem. You're all writers and you have the problem of the competitive ego. There may sometimes be a little envy, a little jealousy, a bit of "If I wrote it, this is the way I'd do it."

Here again, what stands you in good stead? Techniques? No, not for a minute. Your own ability to evaluate—to say, "I know what this man is talking about, and I can use this, or I can't use the other thing." Only to that degree will you be able to work, because in the theater you're constantly dealing with the competitive egos.

To rewrite, you must learn more than just how to write a play. You must learn about acting; you must know how to eliminate three pages of dialogue with a piece of business. This is part of rewriting. In order to be able to rewrite, you must know what an actor can do with a look or a change of voice. You must be able to hear it as well as put it down on paper. You need a knowledge of theater.

The problem of actual production is one of fantastic speed in rewriting—an ability to cut ruthlessly in a scene that you cannot possibly hold on. O'Neill is considered our greatest playwright. I don't hesitate to say that I think his work is overwritten. Most people agree. He refused to cut. He established a reputation where he could refuse to cut. But I don't think this helped his plays.

How do you go about rewriting? No one can tell you. They may say to you, "Go home." Then the director takes over. Young authors have been sent home or told, "Don't come to the theater!" The author comes around and feels, "This is what happened to my play?" Shocked! Hurt. Disturbed. His baby has been killed. But if the baby has been killed, I can assure you, it's the author's fault and not the director's or the producer's. If there are problems in the play, don't just slough them off on these other people. It is you who have failed to do a specific job. So what do the problems of rewriting come down to ultimately? This: How much do you know? How much have you learned about the theater? There are techniques—but what good are they if you don't know how to use them?

QUESTION: The things that an author falls in love with in his play—don't they ever belong there?

MR. KRAMM: Oh, yes. But they aren't always the things that *necessarily* belong there. In the writing of a play, you're so close to it that, as you move along, a thought may occur to you spontaneously, as you're writing, that you'll enlarge and build up out of all proportion to its value to the play. You may not like to take it out, but you must.

QUESTION: Mr. Kramm, I noticed what you said about eliminating a page of dialogue with business. When a writer has an idea of how a particular scene should be done, isn't the director inclined to take out all the directions that the author put in? Must this all go? It's such a part of writing.

MR. KRAMM: It's a phase of writing which the author imagines. But the business may not work in terms of the particular actor who is interpreting. When I directed *The Shrike,* the company with Van Heflin, he read a line in a particular way and I stopped him and he said, "Joe, I'm only following what you have in the script. The business." I said, "Don't pay any attention to what that man put down on paper," because it wasn't right for Heflin. That particular value didn't sound right coming from him as it did coming from Jo Ferrer.

QUESTION: Is there any value to recording your reading?

MR. KRAMM: If you have a tape recorder and you want to read the play aloud, by all means do it. Actors have said to me, "Joe, your stuff is tough to learn, but it plays." Now, the reason for that, from my own point of view, is that I was an actor myself for fifteen or eighteen years and a director long before writing became a factor. I think playing it back on a tape recorder is an excellent idea. You'll learn an awful lot.

QUESTION: If an actor says your stuff plays well, why do you think he finds it tough to learn?

MR. KRAMM: Because before an actor learns to play it, he must learn to think it. At first he hasn't absorbed the thinking process of the character.

He must think like the character, and until he does, the material is difficult to learn, because the actor isn't working with his own mental processes.

QUESTION: Instead of reading it to yourself, if you read it to some other person . . .

MR. KRAMM: Yes, it takes someone else to say, "What's the motivation? What's the reason?" Judging your own work is partly a matter of looking at a line and saying, "Has it been said in the best possible way? Succinctly, briefly?"

I set certain values for myself in a line. It must advance the play. It must be psychologically sound. It must be right for this character. Your characters must think individually, not alike, and your dialogue must advance the play. If the scene doesn't advance the play or if the dialogue doesn't move the play along, then it's of no value.

QUESTION: You mentioned earlier the contributions of the actors and director that can add to a play. Would you elaborate?

MR. KRAMM: I think it's extremely important for writers to take a course in acting and a course in directing. Now it's true there are successful playwrights who've never acted. But you can't deny that certain people have talents beyond the ordinary. Toscanini said of Menuhin, when he heard him play at the age of seven or eight, "And they say all men are born equal!" We're not all born equal; some of us need more learning and technique than others.

Let me stick to the problem of the writer in relation to the actor. First, think in terms of an actor's presence or quality. I teach acting and directing and I do improvisations occasionally in gibberish. Once, we took a scene from *Idiot's Delight* and I had the two actors do the scene in gibberish. And what did we discover? That *the words didn't make a damn bit of difference!* It was the value—what came through them as individuals—that made the scene come alive. An actor contributes what he brings in terms of meaning. This is why writers must not be that precious about words. You must discover what your words convey in feeling, in meaning. Are they moving the thing along? This is why learning something about the acting technique is important.

QUESTION: Then you could write a scenario and let your actors do the rest.

MR. KRAMM: What I say and mean by "gibberish" is that the actors are forgetting the words and playing the action of the scene. They're playing the meaning of the scene. Have you ever watched a play in a foreign language which you didn't understand? The play comes across.

QUESTION: You couldn't do that with Shaw, of course. Where the words do mean something—an intellectual playwright.

MR. KRAMM: Yes, that's a different problem entirely. In Shaw, long scenes go on in which people do nothing but talk to one another, conveying ideas.

QUESTION: But it would hold true for Shakespeare?

MR. KRAMM: It certainly would.

QUESTION: But you wouldn't get the poetry.

MR. KRAMM: You're getting too literal. I'm trying to indicate only this: If you take moments from a play—I'm not saying to do an entire play in gibberish [laughter]—I'm saying take moments and you'll discover that if the actors are playing the *meaning* of the scene, the words don't matter, because you understand what it is that's happening between the characters. Where the quality that the author contributes is essentially an emotional quality, then the words are not that important. Then the meaning and fullness of the emotion is much more important.

QUESTION: Where does the emotion come from if not from words?

MR. KRAMM: No, I beg your pardon—that is a fallacy! I'm sorry!

QUESTION: Well, what is the difference between a well- and a badly written play?

MR. KRAMM: The difference is between the understanding of the people in terms of their thinking and their emotions rather than just the words. Have you never in all your life found yourself in a situation where you were thinking one thing and saying something else? Sometimes you come home tired or hurt and you don't want to talk about it. But you're making conversation that really has nothing to do with what you are thinking. But you could say them and the audience would know because . . .

QUESTION: No one pays admission to hear those words . . .

MR. KRAMM: I beg your pardon! That's exactly what they pay for! I'll get vain and immodest if you like—there's a scene in my play *Build with One Hand* where the man is baiting another man because he feels this other man is superior to him. He's talking about a lot of things that have nothing to do with what he's thinking because he can't come out and say, "You're bigger than I am and I'm afraid of you." So, he goes way around it. It was one of the most successful scenes in the play because the more he talked, the more the audience said, "Oh, this poor man."

QUESTION: So many of us have had disastrous experiences with directors. If you could tell us the positive contributions of the director, it would be useful.

MR. KRAMM: Okay. What the audience sees in the theater is the ultimate responsibility of the director. That seems to eliminate you as authors, but it doesn't at all. The point is that the director's job is to understand you, your play, and your characters as thoroughly as you do. Then, to be able to convey and bring from the actors the performances that will make your play come alive. Now, if you work with a director, whether it's in a rehearsed reading or a Broadway production, your initial reaction will be hostile, because the director comes in and he's going to tell you what he thinks of your play. You're going to sit there and try to be pleasant. You'll bristle at the things he says, or you'll listen with a great deal of understanding, depending on the way he puts it.

The problem of determining whether he really knows the play or not depends entirely on whether you yourself—again it comes down to you—are sure of what your play is saying or whether or not it's what you want it to say. Then, if he talks to you and begins to give you a lot of hogwash of what he thinks the play is, you'll see that this man doesn't know. But if he says, "This is what I think the play is," and it coincides with what you think, then you discover this man isn't trying to redo your play his way, but wants to do *your* play. This is the man to work with.

The problem of working with actors is a very special one. It requires understanding each actor and understanding each character in the play. Actors are individuals and the characters are individuals; the director has to make the two become one. A director who cannot take a suggestion from his actor is unsure of himself. Intelligent actors do have ideas. The actor must not be afraid of the director. You, as the author, must not be afraid of him. It's your job to see that a good relationship is established, because it's your play that's being produced and they're your people that are being presented on the stage. It's your job to see to it that the director always works with the actors to get what you want out of the characters. If he doesn't, you've got to feel free to talk to him.

QUESTION: At what point do you talk to him? Do you give him time to get it set?

MR. KRAMM: Yes. Yet you have the right to talk to him at any time you think it's going wrong. But people's levels of development are different. One actor will come along fast and have the character inside of a week; as the author you may be fooled by it. Another will take longer to come along and you may think, "What's happening? What's wrong? Two weeks of rehearsals now and I don't see the character!" And you get upset and go to the director and he says, "Don't get upset. I know this actor." Then it's a matter of faith.

If other things have come along right, you'll go along with him. Again, the problem is so individual it depends entirely on your own judgment. But *always in relation to your play!* Don't let the director suddenly put something on the stage which is not yours. Now we all know that *Picnic* was a big success—ran for nearly two years on Broadway. But the playwright, Bill Inge, was heartbroken. As far as he was concerned, this was not his play. Some will say, "What the hell! I'll take two thousand dollars a week as long as it's a big success."

Josh Logan, one of the biggest men in the theater, took over *Picnic* with an autocratic hand. Bill Inge had very little to say. The play might have been as big a success done his way. We'll never know. But Logan's interpretation ran for two years. If you're nobody, and you've got Logan—Logan's got the play. If you're nobody and you've got Kazan—Kazan's got the play. But if you're nobody and the director is somebody who's just beginning to make a name, then you're on a level and you can talk to him.

QUESTION: But you shouldn't talk to the actors . . .

MR. KRAMM: No, you shouldn't. Only one person should talk to the actors, and that's the director. There can be only one authority in the theater once the play has gone into rehearsal, and that's the director. The theater is not a democracy.

QUESTION: What if the actor comes to you and wants help . . .

MR. KRAMM: It isn't going to do you much good to tell the actor what you think. The actor has already been rehearsing with his fellow actors in a certain way. If you try changing, the whole cast is going to be affected by it.

MR. HAMLIN: How do you feel about authors being their own directors?

MR. KRAMM: I failed when directing my play *Build with One Hand* because the problems of rewriting and performance became so crucial that I found I was giving a great deal of time to the rewriting and there wasn't enough time to rehearse new material. This was a failing because the play was not ready. *The Shrike*, however, was ready—except for those two scenes—so it didn't present a real problem in terms of directing.

QUESTION: That competitive ego of New Dramatists. Given a choice of fellow playwrights or an assorted theatrical group, who would you want to criticize your play? Playwrights, or just human beings? [Laughter.]

MR. KRAMM: I would say that both professional and nonprofessional opinions are valuable, and that even though the competitive ego inevitably operates when you're working with fellow playwrights, it can still be very valuable to you. The people that I know in the group have told the author what they felt, and those people were able to help. Now it's true there are members who will tear you apart. If you are able to listen to them and say, "Okay, let them tear me apart. They don't bother me. The other criticism I'm getting is sound. I can use it." Don't limit the opportunity of getting criticism for your play to just the professionals. Go to people who are not in the theater at all, because these are the people who will listen as an audience. They will know whether or not they have been pleased, entertained, and moved.

QUESTION: When you bring a play to people like this, what are the questions you put to them? Or do you just sit back and listen to them?

MR. KRAMM: It wouldn't be wise to put questions to the nonprofessionals, for this reason: They will suddenly find themselves on the spot, and they will try to cover up if they didn't like the play. If, for example, they're your neighbors, they're going to want to live with you. They're not going to be completely honest with you. They will say, "I liked some of it. I liked this or I like that . . ."

When I finished the first draft of the first act of *Build with One Hand*, I got some doctors in to hear it. The play happens to deal with doctors, but it's not a medical play. It has to do with doctors as human beings and with the idea of forming a clinic. There are two surgeons and an internist who came to the reading of the first draft of the first act, and they listened, and halfway through the scene—when I started talking about forming a clinic—I could feel the tension in the room. You could cut it with a knife. It was fantastic. From that point on I knew something was wrong, either with the play or with these people. I finished the act and knew it wasn't good. They didn't say a word. They all sat around and looked at each other. They looked at me—complete silence.

The embarrassment was enormous, and finally I said, "Look, I know it's bad. You don't have to say anything. Please don't feel disturbed. We'll have a drink and you don't have to talk about it." Now that reading was extremely valuable to me. I got a great deal from it just having them listen to it, no question about it, particularly in knowing from their silence what was bad.

QUESTION: What about timing?

MR. KRAMM: As you're writing the play I wouldn't be concerned with timing. I would be concerned only with "Am I telling the story?" If you start writing an act and you think, "My God, this thing is getting awfully long," you limit yourself, because you don't give yourself the opportunity to tell the story. Tell your story as you want to tell it, create your characters as fully as you need to create them. When it's finished, cut it down to the normal length.

When you start cutting, you simply cannot say, "Slash here, slash there," because what you are taking out may affect what is left in the play. You may be cutting certain moments that you do not think important. But somewhere in those lines or in that page may be motivation for something you've left in that originated as a result of something that happened before. So when you cut, do so in terms of the entire play. You must make sure that you have not destroyed any particular element, any motivation of the character or any facet of the structure that is necessary to the overall play.

MR. HAMLIN: Thank you very much, Mr. Kramm.

PHOTOGRAPH BY IRVING PENN.

Howard Bay

(1912–1986)

A veritable mill of creativity, the designer Howard Bay contributed to a staggering number of Broadway productions, more than 170 in all. A voracious reader and a man of wide-ranging interests, Bay was noted for his innovations as well as his productivity. In his view, "The designer's cranium is the busy intersection between show business and the fine arts."

In 1960 he won a Tony for the design of *Toys in the Attic*, a drama by his close friend Lillian Hellman. In 1966 he again took the award, this time for the musical *Man of La Mancha*. He also won Donaldson Awards for *Carmen Jones* and *Up in Central Park*.

A man of few words, Bay was once praised by the Boston theater critic Elliot Norton as "one of the few modest men I've ever known in the theater." But in his quiet way he accomplished much. As the dean of American stage designers, he put that honorary title to good use when he founded the stage design department at Brandeis University, where he taught for a number of years. His maxim for recruiting teachers for the design department was: "Don't hire anyone with a Ph.D. Anyone who's spent six to eight years in a library couldn't know much about the theater."

He wrote an acclaimed book, *Stage Design,* a compilation of theory and insights from a life in the practice. And he was a potent force for the betterment of designers. For twenty years he was president of United Scenic Artists, the union of scenic, costume, and lighting designers. His union involvement continued despite his being blacklisted for almost a decade.

Bay strongly believed that playwrights should express themselves without worrying about the set. He was asked once if he preferred working on plays by live authors or classics by dead ones. He answered, "Dead are nicer. The tough live ones were like Elmer Rice and Sidney Kingsley, who had positive, detailed technical ideas. Both were brilliant and nice gentlemen. But they picked up too much backstage stuff."

Among Bay's theatrical credits are *The Merry Wives of Windsor, The Little Foxes, The Moon Is Down, Count Me In, Finian's Rainbow, The Cool World, Look Back in Anger, One Touch of Venus,* and *Come Back, Little Sheba.* His film work includes *Up in Central Park* and *The Exile.* He was designing *The Music Man* for a Peking Opera House production at the time of his death.

A NEW DRAMATISTS CRAFT DISCUSSION

with Howard Bay
December 12, 1956

Miriam Balf introduces Mr. Bay.

MISS BALF: Mr. Bay, are playwrights today using scenic designers to the best advantage?

MR. BAY: Playwrights, per se, create their own little worlds and are apt to literally describe the scenery. They not only show that they're professional craftsmen, but that they tend to box in and make their playwriting very artificial. They should leave it vague and allow the imagination of the designer to help the playwright create the final product. A playwright worries too much about problems in a mechanical sense. More imaginative work would happen if playwrights would state the problem they wished to solve and breeze on in their writing without worrying about the mechanics.

In a commercial sense, certain managements naturally tend to shy away from the script that has thirty-nine changes and fifty-five in the cast. Naturally! But the constriction of writing to fit an economical set is bad thinking for a playwright, because I don't think in the last analysis that any play is ever rejected because of the supposed production cost or mechanical problems.

MISS BALF: Are you suggesting, Mr. Bay, that you can write a play with many sets and it would be viewed with as much favor as a one-set play?

MR. BAY: If you had two scripts, side by side and balanced in the scale, and one could be produced for $50,000 and the other for $100,000, a manager might take the $50,000 item. But I don't think you ever have that mechanical a choice presented.

QUESTION: What is the difference in the production cost between the one-set show and a two- or three-set show?

MR. BAY: Some one-set shows can cost more than some multiscene shows. What is more important is the operating cost of the show during its run.

It's immaterial what a show costs initially. But it is of key importance whether it takes five or ten stagehands to move it for the run of the show. Shortsighted managers who don't yet know their way around think they're getting a bargain if they're getting a cheaply built set but have forgone the extra cost to make it mechanically simple to operate.

Also, the simplicity of operation that economics call for may also solve certain problems on a creative level. For instance, when I did *The Shrike* I was called in to do it the day before rehearsal. I read the script in an hour, had a talk with the management about it in a cab coming back uptown, and I had figured it out. I arrived at it in a negative way. I said for the spirit of the show it's nonsensical to design it in the way it's described in the script.

The whole point of the script was the rigidity of a framework you couldn't escape. But the play went from a ward where things were moved from scene to scene, beds were placed a little differently, an office where things were moved about—in other words, the monotonous sameness of the setting was not made a key question in relation to the show. For that you would have had to have a single rigid framework which you never escaped.

Who can say whether I arrived at the design through economics or aesthetics? Also, I felt that the machinery of taking time to change would dissolve the tension of the show. If the curtain went down and it took twenty, twenty-five, thirty seconds to change the scenery, I thought the tenuous thread of the play would be broken too often. I don't know how to describe my motivations, but the design was proven right the way we did it.

MISS BALF: Could you give us any examples of plays which you thought were not aided by a skeleton set, since it seems to be used indiscriminately?

MR. BAY: Well, personally, I don't think *Death of a Salesman* was aided by its set. There was a curious mixture of styles all in one place. The arbitrariness of the levels was kind of destructive. *The Glass Menagerie* and *A Streetcar Named Desire* were all of a piece.

MISS BALF: Many of us have difficulty in deciding whether our plays should be a realistic set or a skeletonized set. Do you say this decision should be left to the designer?

<u>MR. BAY</u>: I think so. If you state that you want a skeletonized set you're setting up a formalization that you probably decided on arbitrarily.

<u>QUESTION</u>: To what extent do you consult with the playwright, the director, and the producer once you've been commissioned to do the set for a play? And suppose they disagree with you—to what extent is there compromise?

<u>MR. BAY</u>: Usually, in any relationship, there's one strong element. Otherwise there's never a production. You function with the strongest person in the setup. There are large arguments, but it usually works out, and an agreeable compromise is reached. I've never reached an impasse.

<u>QUESTION</u>: Mr. Bay, you mentioned earlier that most playwrights tend to limit the scene designer's function—prescribe and proscribe too much. How would you feel if a playwright sets his play on a bare stage?

<u>MR. BAY</u>: Well, I have reacted to that sort of assignment. [Laughter.] And you discover the playwright didn't really mean it [laughter] as you go along point by point. You find the playwright wants a little bit of aid and support and props. He imagined and wrote a real situation in a real location, composed of objects that are aids to the actors and to the situation involved. There are very few plays in this world so strong that the character writing creates a complete environment.

I'll throw it back at you in that sense. An environment can be created merely in give-and-take between characters. For instance, in *Long Day's Journey into Night,* a very important factor is the house. The values would be lost if you didn't have drowsy summer furniture, or if you didn't feel the fog, if you didn't feel the upstairs. The timing of that show could not be worked out if the exits upstairs weren't behind a barrier that you accept as the way upstairs.

<u>QUESTION</u>: I gather that you would like to have us give you as simple a thing as we can, and let you take over from there. Is that what you mean?

<u>MR. BAY</u>: There may be certain mechanical requirements upon which certain things are predicated. Those should be stated. But the main purpose and best aid to the eventual physical production is the spirit of the

environment. If the designer can't figure it out from reading the dialogue, then there's some deficiency on the part of the designer.

QUESTION: In other words, you like to take it from the dialogue rather than from the description of the mechanics?

MR. BAY: Some scripts for the first reading, I don't read the directions.

QUESTION: Sometimes a playwright writes the set into the play in a way that makes them inseparable. He feels that once his play goes on, it has to have the set he visualized or all is lost. Have you run into that type of playwright?

MR. BAY: Is there another type? [Laughter.] Sure! Naturally! A playwright, in the process of creating a play, must of necessity create what he feels is the one and only world which his people can inhabit. But the theater being a collective affair, he'll find actors who don't look like the people he visualizes. He's going to have a set designer who'll perhaps create something different. He may never like it, or may not like it until it's all together in one piece.

MISS BALF: Did you, Mr. Bay, ever design a set which pleased you mightily and disappointed the playwright?

MR. BAY: I remember a producer hating a set of mine. It was for *Chicken Every Sunday*. It was a ramshackle boarding house in Tucson, Arizona. I made an old Victorian thing with people bouncing around in it. It had a nice tired quality which I thought was right. It helped the humor of the show. But the producer hated it because he'd only produced grade C Westerns and when you said "Arizona" to him, he visualized that adobe where you threw the Navajo rug over the rail sort of thing. [Laughter.]

QUESTION: I find a single set very restricting. Arthur Miller wrote that it takes about a third of the playwright's time just to rationalize the comings and goings of his characters in terms of the one setting. Is there another way of getting out of that one set?

MR. BAY: It depends on the makeup of any given playwright, whether he thinks in terms of the standard Ibsen construction of a play or thinks in episodic fashion. I'm getting a little tired myself of the simultaneous cut aways; you know, upstairs, downstairs, the backyard, and so forth.

QUESTION: If you want to use a couple of rooms and a large area that would be the yard, can you black out these rooms when you just want to use the yard?

MR: BAY: When you lay out that many playing areas across the stage, the visibility demands shallowness. You have to create a very narrow shelf to act on for sight lines. You cannot literally black out every other area, because to get the feeling of sunlight and boisterousness for a couple of scenes, there's an amount of spill-light. If somebody wears a white shirt, the amount of spill-light off it will illuminate this surface, even if it's all black. Blacking out is a relative term. If you have only two areas on a stage, then you can pinpoint down those areas. But if you play a conventional, completely literal three-dimensional sunlight scene, you can't black out for two feet around it.

QUESTION: Often I've seen a play in rehearsal and then seen it with a set and it was much poorer with the set. Is that because scene designers are working at cross-purposes with the playwright, trying to put on what's in their mind instead of something in the audience's minds and emotions?

MR. BAY: It could very well happen. The point is, "imagination" is an awfully loose word in the world. The conditioning of people varies a great deal. When you assume they all have identical imaginations, it places an awful burden on the playwright. One of the designer's primary functions is to try to get a common denominator of understanding so that the imagination of the people is channeled a certain way.

I know what you mean about certain shows that look better in rehearsal. But a set is also a theatrical atmosphere. When the audience comes in and pays its money, it doesn't accept the conventions we do when we go to a run-through. Money's worth in the theater is an important thing.

MISS BALF: How would you explain the success of *Our Town*?

MR. BAY: Well, it's a perfect piece of nostalgia. It's all there—all the trite situations that were ever invented, put in one evening.

MISS BALF: Then you don't need a set to identify it?

MR. BAY: No.

MISS BALF: Would that interest you as a set designer? As a technical problem?

MR. BAY: Yes. That's a good problem. Actually, the movie was well designed too. It didn't detract that they had a collection of literal objects, because they were handled very well. A couple of things gained, I think—a couple of things got a little confused. For instance, the rain in the cemetery gained. You never for one moment in the movie said, "Isn't that clever?" But it was a delicate thing in the theater, done only with umbrellas. You accepted the scene much more readily in the movie.

QUESTION: May I go back to the blackout question for a minute? Suppose, for example, you have a rather dim living room with a piano and in the following scene you want to concentrate on the piano, which is now supposed to be elsewhere. Could you do it by throwing lights on the piano only and blacking out the rest of the living room? Could you depend on the audience's imagination to concentrate where the light leads them?

MR. BAY: It could well happen if the preparation of the segue were handled right, writing-wise and directorial-wise. If there's preparation for handling it smoothly, I don't see why not.

QUESTION: If a playwright could write a play in one set or in six blackout scenes with meager changes of props and furniture, could you give me some idea as to difference in cost? I know you said a playwright shouldn't be bothered with the economic differences between a single and a multiple set.

MR. BAY: I think that's because of what the area of concentration of a playwright should be. If he has to say something, I think it would be peculiar if he didn't go ahead and say it.

QUESTION: But if you can say it in two different ways. Don't playwrights have to face this economic thing, and especially beginning playwrights?

MR. BAY: I think it's backward sort of thinking for a playwright to worry about that as a major problem. There is an erroneous idea, for instance, that the handling of the furniture and the properties is cheaper than the handling of scenery. It's quite the reverse, as a matter of fact. Say you have no walls, no problems except furniture. The changing of that furniture is more difficult than the changing of an acreage of canvas. Your gridirons and fly systems can take flats up and down like that! But to move the whole floor plan with furniture attached is mechanically far more difficult.

QUESTION: Suppose you had a play in which a crowd was an influence, and yet you couldn't get the crowd on the stage. Could you project a motion picture of a crowd and get the desired effect?

MR. BAY: No, it's a very dangerous and ticklish affair. Films and projections are both a separate world. You might use a projection in the theater in a very formal sense, like we did in *The Living Newspaper*. There we'd say, "Well, anything we want to use, we'll use." But that's a format that you'd devise whole, and it's accepted from the word go.

But when you use the projections or movies in the theater, then they have a life of their own. There's a no-man's-land that separates it from the acting area. To augment normal-type drama with projections that are positive or with film would take the unity of a frame and throw it away.

MISS BALF: To illustrate the thing that Mr. Bay is saying, Williams planned *The Glass Menagerie* originally with titles to be flashed on a screen and the director took them out.

MR. BAY: Projections and stuff may become pretentious. That's why musicals are interesting to me. You create a show and the elements can be from left field.

MISS BALF: You mean you can be more imaginative about a musical?

MR. BAY: The satisfaction of working on a good play is a great satisfaction. But as to a mediocre script—I'd rather work on a mediocre musical.

QUESTION: Mr. Bay, what was your last judgment on the set you did for *Night of the Auk*? How did you regard that set by the time of the opening?

MR. BAY: Well, I liked it. [Laughter.]

QUESTION: I got the feeling that the acting was blocked by the set.

MR. BAY: You had a large set; the actors, six-foot men, were projected into your laps. Full-scale people. So they were never surrounded by anything that dwarfed them. Of course they couldn't escape from the rigidity of the mechanism. That's the point of it—they even say it in words in the show.

QUESTION: The set was terribly exciting. But the characters wearing trousers and shirts the same color as the set—to me, they were kind of lost in the set.

MR. BAY: We had some dark, contrasting costumes. But they looked like costumes. So we underplayed it. When you have the playwright's poetry going like crazy, you want to underplay anything you can. That's why we took it back to ordinary fatigues, to give the people a more workaday look.

MISS BALF: What is the advantage of a raked stage, Mr. Bay?

MR. BAY: It has a distinct advantage: No one is ever deadly dull standing planted on a stage, like us sitting here. You don't get that feeling of inactivity. There is a certain tension and fluidity on a raked stage.

QUESTION: I'm amazed that none of the actors object because, much as I liked the set, I had the feeling the actors were on a sort of obstacle course, where one misstep could lead to a broken leg.

MR. BAY: Well, it's a good thing they had that to do, isn't it? [Laughter.]

QUESTION: How many levels did you have in that set, Mr. Bay?

MR. BAY: Seven.

QUESTION: Mr. Bay, isn't the tendency today to play things in levels, restricting playing space on the stage?

MR. BAY: Yes. You get a feeling after a while that you are restricted. Too many things are required to be on stage at one time.

QUESTION: Mr. Bay, you say you like to work on a play from the ground up, so to speak. When would you like to be brought into the whole picture?

MR. BAY: As much in advance as possible. But the economics of production are such that everything telescopes. I don't know whether there's any way to avoid it. The last money doesn't come in until a few weeks prior to rehearsal, and then everything has to go full speed in many directions. Often you don't have time for the leisurely conferences you ought to have with the director and the writer.

MISS BALF: Do you think too many of us tend to use the drawing—or living—room when we might set our play more imaginatively?

MR. BAY: I don't think so. Playwrights think in terms of drawing rooms. They're drawing-room playwrights, let's face it. [Laughter.]

MISS BALF: Mr. Bay, is there any word of advice that you, as a scenic designer, would like to give to the playwright?

MR. BAY: No! [Laughter.] Playwrights often worry about small mechanical details rather than the large ideas.

QUESTION: If *Night of the Auk* had run, you'd have had a very low operating cost, wouldn't you?

MR. BAY: Yes, two electricians, the head and the assistant, who worked both the board and the sound; the one prop man; and the curtain man. That's all.

QUESTION: What will happen to that set?

MR. BAY: There's a little operator who decided it would look swell in Palisades Amusement Park in a tent. The kids will put in the nickels and play with all the gadgets.

MISS BALF: I've heard of buying tables from sets, and lamps, but that's the first time I've ever heard of the whole set being bought.

QUESTION: What is the pay scale of stagehands? It's important, since we're talking about expenses.

MR. BAY: I'd say the average is about $115 a week. The producer pays that. The real economics is that the theater gets about 35 percent of the box office!

MISS BALF: The theater itself? You mean the theater owner?

MR. BAY: Yes.

MISS BALF: So it's the real-estate operator who wins! [Laughter.] Thank you very, very much, Mr. Bay.

PHOTOGRAPH BY RALPH A. ROGERS.

Mary Drayton

(1905–1994)

Mary Drayton's story is not only about what she accomplished. Hers is the experience of most artists in the theater—a life of determined striving, often blocked by setbacks, yet still highlighted by moments of triumph and fulfillment.

Born and bred in Hope, Arkansas, she dreamed of a glamorous life on the New York stage. At the age of twenty she left Hope and landed in the big city. There she earned her master's degree in English literature from Columbia University, was a model, a singer—she sang at the 1939 World's Fair in New York—and an actress.

Ms. Drayton appeared on Broadway in *Few Are Chosen, On Location,* and *Thanks for Tomorrow.* She also understudied Katharine Cornell in the national tour of *No Time for Comedy,* where she met her future husband, the actor Tom Helmore. This promising career was tragically altered, however, in 1945 when she suffered a broken back in a bus accident. Forced to scale back her acting, she turned to writing.

Her first play, originally titled *Salt of the Earth* (adapted from the novel *The Peaceable Kingdom*), was a comedy about bigamy in the Mormon community. It was performed in summer stock and later remounted as *Second Fiddle* in La Jolla, California, with Teresa Wright.

Another play, *Debut*, became Drayton's first Broadway offering in 1956, starring Mr. Helmore and Inger Stevens. Her next play, *Build Me a Bridge*, an examination of race relations in her native Arkansas, received a rousing reception at the Cleveland Playhouse. She was back on Broadway in 1966 with *The Playroom*, a thriller about rich New York teenagers. An immediate success, it was made into an MGM movie for which Ms. Drayton wrote the screenplay.

Her last play, *Ducks in a Row*, was done in Santa Fe, New Mexico, in 1984 with Don Murray starring. The last thing Ms. Drayton wrote was a novel titled *All Our Secrets*. *The Playroom* is still produced throughout the country, and *All Our Secrets* remains in print.

A NEW DRAMATISTS CRAFT DISCUSSION

with **Mary Drayton**
May 5, 1956

**Miss Drayton's play *Debut* had opened on Broadway a few weeks
before and members of the New Dramatists had been
invited to a run-through.**

MISS DRAYTON: I would never say to anybody, nor would I ever feel like
saying, "I told you so." But it is something to have had your own negative judgment of your play confirmed by the critics. Had I believed pas-
sionately in the play and in its merits, obviously I would have quite a
different attitude toward it from the one I have now. It means something
to me to feel that my initial judgment about it was, according to the critics, the correct one.

QUESTION: Did you feel that any of the critics put it unfairly?

MISS DRAYTON: There was a kind of viciousness about some of them
which I felt was probably because I had been an actress. You know,
actors are never supposed to be able to do anything, ever. I started out to
be an actress, then I was hurt in an accident and didn't get to go on with
my acting career. Some of the press releases said I had been an actress. I
got a feeling that may have colored it.

Debut is the second play I wrote. I wrote one five years ago, which
was called *Salt of the Earth*. I'd been out on the Coast and Tom [Hel-
more, her husband] came back to do a play. I read the play and thought
there was a wonderful part in it for me. I actually thought I had it. I
came back here to do it and found I didn't have it. Subsequently, I found
out that the girl who got the part had an investment in the play, so . . .
[Laughter.]

Next, friends gave me a book to read called *The Peaceable Kingdom*.
I'd never read anything about the Mormons. It was a wonderful character story, and I thought there was a play in it. I said to Tom, "There's a
play in this, and I know this woman is a fabulous character." He read it
and said, "There's no play in it—nobody could make a play out of it." I

said, "I know there's a play in it. I even think I could make a play of it." So I wrote this play and gave it to Miriam Howell [Ms. Drayton's agent] to read, and it was sold the first week she had it! There were several people interested in buying it! Boy, this is easy! [Laughter.]

Well, the scene changes. We're in Boston with *Salt of the Earth* and we play more for comedy. We've cast wrong for that, so we don't come in to New York.

Right after that closed, my agent called me and said, "A man called me and wanted me to recommend someone to do an adaptation of a book called *Maria and the Captain*. Have you read it?" I said, "No." She sent it to me. I read it and called her and I said, "Nobody could do an adaptation of this." [Laughter.] She said, "Well, I think you should go and talk to this man. His name is Mr. William Dozier. He's one of the vice presidents of CBS." I said, "I'll meet anybody who thought I could make a play out of this."

So, I went over to see him and left Tom in a bar downstairs, expecting to join him in about fifteen minutes. Hours later I was still in Bill Dozier's office, by which time I could see it all pretty clearly. He said I didn't have to do anything about sticking to the book at all. [Laughter.] In other words, he sold me a bill of goods; let's face it.

He did have an idea which I liked. I could throw the book out the window, and I could have a man going down South, a Republican, trying to sell Eisenhower—this was during the Eisenhower campaign for president—to a yellow-dog Democrat down South. Well, having been brought up down there and having had a father who was a yellow-dog Democrat, I thought that I could have a lot of fun with it. Get a lot of things off my chest that I had been wanting to say about the South for many years and write a kind of political spoof, really rib the South, a tongue-in-cheek thing to expose a lot of things.

Bill didn't have any idea of how to do it—nothing at all. I spent five weeks on it. I used one incident from the book, not the way it was treated in the book—I even changed the names of the characters. I sent a copy to Bill Dozier and he was very pleased with it. He gave me a thousand dollars. I sent a copy to Miriam with this request: I had an idea of a double ending. I thought if Eisenhower won, we could end it one way; if Adlai Stevenson won, we could end it another way. I even had an idea for a publicity thing which was rather crazy, and I wanted

Miriam to send a script to Dick Maney [a prominent press agent] to see what he thought of it from a publicity angle.

Well, I finished the script on a Thursday, and Miriam gave it to Maney on Saturday. He called her right up and said, "This is hilarious. It must be done immediately, and I have taken it into my own hands and have sent it to Otto Preminger to read." Otto read it on the weekend.

On Tuesday morning, Bill Dozier and I had breakfast with Otto at the St. Regis. He had already persuaded Bill, by the time we'd left there, to let him and Aldrich and Myers [coproducers], who also read it over the weekend—it must have been a hot little script! [laughter]—to come in and produce it with him, with Otto directing. I asked Bill when I first met him, "Do you have the money? I'm not going to go into this just for speculation and a thousand dollars." He said, "Oh, I have the money. Don't worry about that."

Well, when we left Otto I told him, "Bill, this is going to delay things." (because I had agreed to go to California to work on the script with Otto). Bill said, "Yes, it will delay things." But it also meant that we had reputable producers and Otto was going to make *The Moon Is Blue*—the movie. Bill felt that we were in very good hands. I said, "Well, it may be very difficult to explain the South to Otto Preminger." [Laughter.] He said, "Well, I think you should try. I think we have to do this."

I must admit that it was a kind of exciting Tuesday morning, to suddenly think that on Thursday I'd be on my way to California. It all sounded very big, with Aldrich and Myers and Otto Preminger! I'd just finished the play on Thursday! [Laughter.] You can forgive me for being a little bit swept up. On Thursday I went to California. And for three weeks I tried to explain the South to Otto Preminger. It would have taken a great deal longer. [Laughter.] It's hard to explain to anybody! And to a Viennese, it's even more remote.

After three weeks I realized I was just spending their money and having a nice time, but I was also a wife and mother. I called Bill and said, "Look, I can't work with Otto. We just kind of argue and nothing happens, and he has the idea that I must take all the politics out and substitute sex for everything from start to finish." I said, "I admit that may be very good box office, but that isn't what we started out to do, which was to try to get a play on in time to capitalize on the presidential election." So Bill said, "All right, come on back and do it your own way."

I took Otto's suggestions up to a point where I could understand what we were talking about, and I did some rewriting. We missed the time that fall when we should have come in, so I realized that I would have to do even more than I thought. However, Otto in his contract was supposed to be ready to go into production when we were ready. Well, when I was ready he was right in the middle of directing the movie of *The Moon Is Blue*, so he couldn't be with us. I told Bill Dozier that I thought that might be fine. [Laughter.] Why didn't we see if we could get another director who might know a little more about the South?

By this time, the play was so sexy that I was worried about whether it was in good taste or not. So I suggested that Miriam Howell send it to Guthrie McClintic. [Laughter.] No! I think Guthrie has excellent taste, and that if there were anything questionable in it, Guthrie would say, "Look, Mary, don't. This is going too far." And so I sent it to him. The next day, much to my surprise, Stanley Gilkey [McClintic's general manager] called me and said, "Mary, Guthrie is crazy about your play and wants to direct it." So I said, "Wonderful. I couldn't be happier," and I called Bill Dozier and said, "Evidently it isn't too objectionable, because Guthrie wants to do it." Bill said, "Fine." We got organized. Donald Oenslager drew sets; Guthrie put on another girl in his office; we started casting; we ran movies, we did everything.

We were within a week of rehearsal when Bill Dozier told us he didn't have the money. This was Bill's first Broadway production and, you see, when we broke off with Otto, we also broke off with Aldrich and Myers and it was just Bill who was producing now. And Stanley had asked me if Bill had the money, and I said, "Yes. He told us all along that he has the money. Talk to Miriam about it." So Stanley talked to Miriam about it and she said, "Oh, yes, Bill assured us since June (this was February) that he had the money."

Bill had been relying on four people each to give him twenty-five thousand dollars. Obviously, around some table over a cocktail, they had said, "Look, Bill, if you find a script you can always count on twenty-five thousand dollars." He counted on them and only one of them came through.

So big things came out in the newspapers about *Debut* being withdrawn for script revisions, maybe for a summer tryout. Their publicity man put all the blame on the script, when there was never even any question about one word of rewrite on anything.

Debut took the rap there, and it was the first black mark against the play. From now on, I am going to be very careful in my first dealings with producers, speaking with them about any announcements that come out in the papers. Whether the play goes on or whether it doesn't, the truth of the thing should come out insofar as possible so that nobody gets blamed needlessly.

QUESTION: How can you help doing that?

MISS DRAYTON: You can. George Nichols sent me a press release on everything that went out about *Salt of the Earth*. I got it first and if I did not want it, I could veto it before anything went out. But that was my first play. I didn't do it on the second one. That's how smart I am!

That summer, Elmer Rice was doing *Salt of the Earth* with Betty Field. They had a resident director at the Poconos in Pennsylvania. He was going to direct it. *Second Fiddle* is what I called *Salt of the Earth* this time.

And John O'Shaughnessy [the director] said, "Look, there's another play of yours I'm very interested in and I'd like to do it. It's a play called *Debut!*" I said, "You didn't have to tell me that because I've only written two." [Laughter.] I said, "Where can we get a girl?" He said, "How about Peggy Ann Garner?" I said, "I've never seen her do anything but *A Tree Grows in Brooklyn*, and that certainly wouldn't make me feel she could do Maria." John said, "She's a brilliant comedienne."

I called Bill Dozier and said, "Look, we have a chance to try this play out here, and I'll do it if you'll guarantee it is a pre-Broadway deal. I don't feel that any play gets a fair shake in summer stock. If you're going to go from place to place and we get a chance to work on it, then maybe you've got a better chance than you do if it's just two weeks' rehearsal and one week playing." Bill said, "Oh, no, if we can get the right setup and the right cast there and everything, we will definitely bring it in." I said, "How about the money?" He said, "Don't worry about the money." [Laughter.]

"Well, we did it. Peggy Ann *did* prove to be a brilliant comedienne and the play was a success. But I saw at that point, what I had was a halfway thing. I had not given up all the satire; in losing some of the political stuff, I had brought the characters a bit more toward reality. The thing had a little bit more substance as a finished story. At the Poconos we rehearsed two weeks, played one week. The man who had the theater in Andover, New

Jersey, came out and saw it and said, "I will hold my season over one week, keep it open one week longer in order to do *Debut* if you will come out and open the Empress Theatre in St. Louis for two weeks out there."

Bill and I thought this would be fine. Then it turned out that Bill didn't send a set man out there; he wasn't going to use the set in the Poconos, and nothing about a New York production was happening—but nothing! That's when my ulcer started.

The result was that we played four weeks that summer. We recast in New York for certain parts. We got Roddy McDowell for Dabney, Kathleen Comages for Aunt Phoebe. We improved the cast. We went to St. Louis and still I was being promised that we were going to bring it in to New York. But day after day nothing happened about a New York production. Nothing at all. I came back and put the play in a trunk and said, "The HELL with it!" I had an ulcer, and that was that.

Nearly a year went by, and one day we were talking about the play with Andy McCullough and Bethel Leslie, who live in the same building, and Andy said he'd like to read it. He read it, fell in love with it, and said—you have no idea how many times this had been said to me!—"Mary, you've got a million dollars here!" [Laughter.] You'll be interested to know that I made $272. [Laughter.] But Andy said, "Mary, you've got to do just a little work on it and everything'll be fine." So I said, "Fine, who am I to turn down a million dollars?"

When I finished I gave it to him. He called me up and said, "I'm crazy about it, I want to buy it." I said, "Okay, it's yours for a dollar fifty." He said, "I'm not kidding. Mike Wallace and I want to put it on." He came up. What he wanted to do with it was to throw out the satire and make it real—play it for comedy, but for real. Let the story carry it. Well, I said, "Andy, it can't be done. It's not possible." I had had this same argument with Otto; I didn't have that same argument with John O'Shaughnessy. He and Guthrie and I saw it the same way. Andy McCullough and I did not see it the same way at all.

So I stuck to my guns. I said, "I cannot do it, Andy. I just couldn't put all that work into it because I do not believe it will ever stand as a story. I think the boys are through letting the boy-meets-girl get by, unless it's done with such a definite point of view that it is clear from the time the curtain goes up that you're saying something about somebody, and not just telling a silly little story."

"No, no!" he said. "You have wonderful characters here."

"I'm sorry," I said, "I simply couldn't do it that way." And I got upset because I had done some work on it.

When he left I said, "I'm terribly thankful." But it kept coming back to me, coming back and back. "Who are you? Here is a production! They want to do it. These are fresh minds. You've had all this trouble with it. It's a script that has a bad mark against it. How do you know that it will ever be done?" I remembered that audiences loved it. They loved it in the Poconos, they loved it for two weeks in St. Louis, which is an urban audience. Now, even by that time some of the satire had been lost, because the first version—which was never done—was the one that Dick Maney liked.

By this time I took a lot of the satire away when I cut all the politics out. So I thought, "Maybe I'm wrong. Who am I? These people think it's better." So I called Andy up and I said, "I've thought it over, and if you're still interested I'll try to do what I think you want." Fine. I did it. They were delighted. They loved it, they adored it.

They were a new producing firm. They said they thought they could raise the money if I would let them do it in stock first. I had sworn I would never have another play done in stock [laughter], but I said, "Fine! Go right ahead. But do not do it anywhere they have a bar in connection with the theater." [Laughter.] So I said, "Some really good summer stock company, you know, at Dennis or Westport or Poconos, or someplace—not any of these places where you get no work done."

All right, fine. It turned out we did it at Matunuck, where there is a large bar [laughter]—a nightclub connected with it. However, I will say they gave us an excellent production, and I do not feel that the bar had anything to do with what happened the other night on Broadway. Not at all.

QUESTION: Who directed it in Matunuck?

MISS DRAYTON: Andy McCullough. I had not known this was going to happen, because Andy had no reputation as a director. I had no reputation as a playwright; Mike and Andy had none as producers. They were going to try to get a name director to bolster it up a little bit. But I was in California in June. When I came back I was told Andy was going to direct it for stock.

He and I did not see eye to eye about the direction, about a great deal of the casting, about practically any of it! The fact remains that it was done in Matunuck very successfully. They did terrific business with it; we got wonderful notices from everybody. On the *Variety* notice alone, they raised seventy-five thousand dollars in four days. So they were set up and ready to go. So I thought, "Fine, everything is okay. We'll just get a director and really go."

Not at all! After the Matunuck thing they called me in for another one of those meetings, and they said they wanted to rewrite the whole thing. They wanted to make it cornier than ever; they wanted me to rewrite Wynn so he's a boy from the wrong side of the tracks, that kind of corny deal. I said, "No."

They forgot to sign Marjorie Steele, who had made quite a hit. She was offered the Van Druten play. She had called me half-a-dozen times for three days from the Coast asking me whether or not she should go into the Van Druten play, and I said, "How can I tell you not to go into it? They want so much from me, and I don't know when I'm going to be able to do it. If you've got a chance to do *Dancing in the Chequered Shade,* you'd better do it." So she did it.

By this time we had no leading lady, and their option was nearly up. We went to a meeting where the fists were flying, practically. And I finally said I wouldn't renew the option. I didn't renew it. Then there was a thing in the paper saying they had given up the option because of disagreements with the author over casting and rewrite. So that was another black eye for *Debut.* I think all those things had to do with the subsequent notices.

The day after they dropped their option, the phone rang. It was Dick Horner. He had read it in the summer; his wife had read for one of the parts; he was crazy about the play; he wanted to buy it.

Finally, since several people wanted it, I said, "I have no sense about these things. You're my agent, Miriam. I rely upon you about which one to let it go to." She decided, instead of taking the experienced producers, to give it to Dick Horner. I must say I don't blame her. I think he's excellent, and I think one day he will be a really fine producer. I gave it to him; we were cast; he did not have a director. John Gerstad had seen it at Matunuck. I had spent a day with him on the beach afterwards and he hadn't mentioned it, so I thought he obviously hated it. It turned out that he liked it very much and wanted to do it, and didn't mention it because Andy McCullough was around and he felt that Andy's direction was all wrong.

It wasn't easy to get a director in November, so when we found that Johnny wanted to do it, Dick was delighted. I was delighted. We got together and I talked with him about it, in a very general way. In too general a way! That's one of the things I've learned. We got into rehearsals, and he rehearsed the actors very well. I felt, however, that his attack on the play was not what it should be. He was directing it for farce. I thought that since we were all committed now to something besides satire, our only chance was to do it tongue-in-cheek so that from beginning to end the audience could tell that it was a spoof, kidding the magnolia and jasmine routine. Well, that was not coming through in the direction.

I talked with John about it; he was extremely amenable, very cooperative. He was handicapped by the fact that we had three inexperienced people in the company—the Maria, the Dabney, and the Marjorie. He had to spend a tremendous amount of time with them. I think the play suffered from that. He got off on the wrong foot with Maria. He began directing her with business, cute and clever things to do. At the run-through we saw that there were no characters there at all. John had directed her with a lot of embellishments on nothing. He had to switch his method after the run-through, which the New Dramatists saw.

So in about two days she had a completely new characterization—a new idea and everything. He had a great many problems. You saw the results. It would have gotten a better press had it been done a little bit better, in casting and direction. If we had gotten mixed notices, I believe we would have found an audience. If I ever write a really good play one day, I do not expect audiences to like it any better than they liked *Debut*. The night we closed we got bravos.

QUESTION: How was it in Matunuck?

MISS DRAYTON: It was better, mainly because the Maria was better. The point of view comes over better if you have a girl who is a person with a problem. Then the whole thing doesn't sound so thin. The jokes are still there about the South, but you can understand them. I was surprised when the critics here didn't even know I was trying to kid the South. When it was done in a romantic way, the comedy seemed to stand out;

whereas, when it was directed all out, hell-bent-for-leather, then the comedy seemed feeble.

QUESTION: Mary, did you ever consider replacing your star or director after the run-through?

MISS DRAYTON: In Boston one of the producers wanted to get rid of our star; the other one wanted to get rid of the director. I had to be the one to decide. I did neither. I had gone through so much with it that I simply couldn't fight any longer. I had a feeling of resignation. Because while all this was happening, audiences were loving it. Also by this time my perspective on it was way off! I'd seen too many versions. This was the fifth one.

I forgot to mention this: When we didn't come in to New York and I got the ulcer—before I put the play in the trunk—I decided to have a panel on it. I told the panel my problem, that everybody had tried to get me to throw out the tongue-in-cheek, kidding stuff, the poking fun at the South, take that all away and just write for story. And they agreed, every one of them, that I was absolutely right in sticking to my guns keeping it a satire, or whatever you call it—a spoof.

QUESTION: You think that if you hadn't gotten off with Preminger at the beginning . . .

MISS DRAYTON: I think we would have had a hit.

QUESTION: He wanted a completely different thing, but you didn't go along with it . . .

MISS DRAYTON: He wanted me to tone down the politics. He said this: "You have written a play that undoubtedly will be a hit. But it is limited to the present situation, which was a political campaign year." He was absolutely right about that. He said, "Take out a lot of politics, build up your characters where there is a relationship between them, and put in sex—then you'll have stock rights, movie—everything like that." But I still feel that had we gone into production then, in September, as we planned, I think we could have had a play which would have run. It was a better play than the one that got on here.

This is an important thing to realize: No matter how much a director has studied a script, he still doesn't know it as well as you do. I think you are liable to feel, because you agree on a few different things, that you are seeing eye to eye on everything. That is what happened with John Gerstad and me. Not that we didn't see eye to eye on things once we got them talked out, but it was just that he had not thought about the things. That's why I think it is terribly valuable for an author and a director to go through, if possible, every line in the play. Maybe I'll never have another director, but if I do, I guarantee that he and I will know exactly what and where a certain scene is going, where a certain character is going, where the whole play is going!

QUESTION: Did you ever lose your objectivity, and if so, how did you regain it? I mean, did it begin to flatten out—the lines, the humor, and the situation—even though at one time you thought it was rich in humor?

MISS DRAYTON: I never thought it was funny. I suppose I got a kick out of it from that standpoint when John O'Shaughnessy directed it in the Poconos. When you get your first reaction and big laughs in summer stock, you know, smallish house and a big yuck comes, then there's a certain satisfaction. But after that, there was too much happening production-wise for me to ever pay too much attention to it script-wise, if that's what you mean?

QUESTION: But doesn't it often happen that, hearing the same scene repeated over and over again, your senses become dulled so that you accept another version than you originally had in mind?

MISS DRAYTON: That's probably what happened. After Matunuck, John wanted certain things done. I put them in at the first run-through. We were about twenty-five minutes long, so John came back afterwards and said, "Mary, you'll have to cut out about twenty-five minutes. I'm frank to say that the things you must cut out are the things that I told you to put in." So, I just cut it right out [laughter] and we went right back to what we had.

QUESTION: Mary, this is going to bring you an income for a long, long time. If it's any consolation, I think that this is an ideal—dirty word—stock play.

MISS DRAYTON: Well, I hope so! The notices were so bad. But they want to do it in Germany and Holland, and I'll be delighted for them to do it anywhere. [Laughter.]

QUESTION: Did I understand you to say that one of the things that you were glad of is the fact that you could rewrite according to someone else's ideas?

MISS DRAYTON: And not fall to pieces when you're not writing what you believe, because you were outvoted, or you may not know which way to go. There must be times when you have to write "to order," don't you think so?

QUESTION: Mary, this is one of the most important things in the entire talk. You had a play and you finished up with no play. Now we all of us have to learn to rewrite, and we all try to rewrite before the production. We know that in a production we may be required to make changes. But the question always is: Should we make changes when we don't believe in them?

MISS DRAYTON: I'll tell you this! Even having taken the beating I have about this, I'm not at all sorry that I did go along. I feel now I might have a little bit more confidence in my own judgment, mainly because I figure that the critics could take it the way they did. You see, I did practically no rewriting while we were in production. I did my rewriting from a calculated compromise I made with myself. I cannot get this play produced the way I want it done. I can get it produced by writing a boy-meets-girl thing, using the material I have. Well, that's a challenge, too. I must admit that every producer I had was very pleased with what I did, which meant that I understood what they wanted.

QUESTION: Maybe you should have stuck to your guns and said to Mr. Preminger, "I'm sorry. Maybe I would have had a hit play, but I wanted to write a play tongue in cheek about the South and I'll stand for it . . ."

MISS DRAYTON: Right! But don't forget, I was sitting at home very happy when my agent called me and told me that a man wanted a book adapted. This was nothing [laughter] that I wanted to do. This man paid me a thousand dollars to do this. [Laughter.] This is quite a different thing . . .

QUESTION: I feel what you have done is much more valuable. Unless it was something that came from your heart . . .

<u>MISS DRAYTON</u>: Yes. If it was something I really cared about, I'd be inclined to agree. Don't forget, I've had three different productions out of it! I've worked with five different directors; I've written five different scripts on this one thing. I've had a complete bust. But at the same time . . .

<u>QUESTION</u>: Mary, where was the original author in all this?

<u>MISS DRAYTON</u>: Oh, she loved it! [Laughter.] She adored it! [Laughter.] She was very cute about it. She said, "How in the world did you ever make such a charming bit of nonsense out of that old sticky book of mine?"

<u>QUESTION</u>: Mary, you have crystallized one thing in my mind. Even though you think your director knows what you mean, it's a good idea to have a chance to go over every line.

<u>MISS DRAYTON</u>: It is essential. A great many plays don't have a chance of success because the director and the author do not understand each other. The sooner the barriers are down between author and director—the sooner you are on a basis of two people working toward a single end—the better for the play. You must be talking in friendly language to another person who wants the play to be a success as much as you do. Then you can get together. This I'm sure of.

PHOTOGRAPH COURTESY OF DAVID WREN.

Joshua Logan

(1908–1988)

Josh Logan often proclaimed, "My life and breath is the theater."

Born in Texarcana, Texas, he saw his first professional play in Shreveport, Louisiana, when he was eight. "As I stepped into the lobby, I was jolted by love at first sight." He never lost the feeling.

In his first year at Princeton, he was invited to act with Henry Fonda, Jimmy Stewart, Margaret Sullavan, and others in the University Players, a summer theater company on Cape Cod. In his senior year, he studied with Konstantin Stanislavsky at the Moscow Art Theater. The master taught him this lesson: "Cherish the fresh; avoid the rigid. Keep working on yourself to learn what's inside. Love the art in yourself, rather than yourself in the art."

Logan's first Broadway job was as sixth stage manager on Howard Lindsay's production of *She Loves Me*. The first show he directed on Broadway lasted only two weeks, but he was a Broadway director at twenty-six. When he was given *Knickerbocker Holiday* (1938) by Maxwell Anderson and Kurt Weill, its great success established him as a top director. By the late 1930s he was directing two or three productions a year. Then came *Charley's Aunt,* starring José Ferrer (1940). As Logan later acknowledged, "If there was any one show that made me famous, it was that one."

Early in World War II, Logan was in the army doing KP when he heard his name boomed over the loudspeaker. He had been selected by Irving Berlin to direct his all-soldier revue *This Is the Army.*

On his return from the service came Berlin's *Annie Get Your Gun* starring Ethel Merman (1946), then Anita Loos' *Happy Birthday* starring Helen Hayes (1946) and *John Loves Mary* by Norman Krasna (1947). Two enduring hits followed with Logan as both coauthor and director: *Mister Roberts*, based on the book by Thomas Heggen (1948); then *South Pacific* with book by Oscar Hammerstein and Logan and music by Rodgers and Hammerstein (1949).

Logan's own play, *The Wisteria Trees*, inspired by his experiences with the Moscow Art Theater production of *The Cherry Orchard* appeared in 1950. His other works include (as director, coauthor, and coproducer) *Wish You Were Here* (1952); (as director and coproducer) *Picnic* (1953) by William Inge; (as director and producer) *Middle of the Night* (1956) by Paddy Chayefsky; (as director and coproducer) *The World of Suzie Wong* (1958); (as director) *Mr. President* (1962), book by Howard Lindsay and Russel Crouse and songs by Irving Berlin.

Films Logan directed include *Picnic* (1956), *Sayonara* (1957), *South Pacific* (1958), *Tall Story* (1960), *Fanny* (1961), *Camelot* (1957), and *Paint Your Wagon* (1969).

A New Dramatists Craft Discussion

with Joshua Logan

January, 1952

Michaela O'Harra introduces Mr. Logan.

MR. LOGAN: Miss O'Harra told me I might start tonight by talking about my recent trip around the world and how it affected my playwriting. She sort of scared me, because I just got off the plane a couple of days ago and it hasn't affected my playwriting at all! [Laughter.]

I had just finished doing a job in London—*South Pacific*—the one that got all the bad notices. We started around the world to forget about all that. As to the theater, we found it was very difficult to find anything as dramatic in the theater as we found on the street. Everything, it seemed to me, was made up of props and scenery, the most exciting props you've ever seen in your life! Then you'd go to the theater and it would all seem kind of tame—just that old story of boy getting girl.

Except for the Kabuki theater I saw in Tokyo. It's difficult to describe because it's very difficult to realize what a wonderful, modern, fresh, exciting theater this is in a place which you hardly know exists. The stage is about sixty feet wide—I believe the biggest of ours is fifty feet wide—so that there is this enormous expanse of scenery. It's a combination of realism, stylization, dance, song and music, drama, melodrama, comedy, properties, scenery and more scenery. If you want a cherry orchard, you have a cherry orchard with trees, cherries, blossoms. If you want a bridge, you have a bridge you could climb over, with a river underneath—a canvas cloth painted like a river with the waves on it.

It's a terribly exciting thing—a riverbank with a bridge, cherry trees, Japanese ladies walking by. Actually, they are men with these elaborate wigs and wonderful kimonos which they hold in a special way. They are very careful in the way they use their hands and see that the kimono doesn't drag behind them until they get inside on the matted floor, where they let it go. Then they move with those sleeves, always remembering how to keep the sleeves from knocking over the tea. That's part of the playwriting.

As this curtain went up, you saw the riverbank and these lovely Japanese ladies walking by on those funny little stiltlike shoes. They slip out of them when they step into the house, because they never wear shoes in a house. You see Japanese life by seeing a play. There's a horse in the stable, a white horse that's just moving slightly so that you're not quite sure whether it's a real horse. Between the horse and the bridge there are two Japanese girls serving tea. Behind them are two figures in black tights and masks, black hoods with black gloves and black sticks in their hands. Tied to the ends of the sticks are two doves, wings outspread—stuffed doves. These men shake the sticks so that the doves fly around the heads of the women as they walk.

I wanted to stand up and yell. This would be a *smash* here. There was something about the combination of reality and unreality and naïveté. We weren't supposed to know that those two men and those two doves . . . Or we *were* supposed to know and who cared?

There are comedies and dramas. Some playwrights who understand Japanese complain that they don't bother very much about making things believable. They just say it—"One hates another"—outright without bothering about why they hate them. But it's beautiful and exciting. You know they've had a revolving stage since before America was discovered.

QUESTION: Would you say that the things you learned in this stimulating experience are applicable to your general direction of American theater?

MR. LOGAN: I somehow feel that in some former reincarnation, I was a Kabuki director. [Laughter.] Kabuki is so close to my feeling about combining visual and tonal elements which can be used to illuminate an idea or an emotion.

This seemed to be a thing I could aim for in directing. It was a little larger than life, and I believe in that. Somebody before used the word "farce" in connection with *Mister Roberts*. It was the idea that I had done some outrageously unbelievable things that had nothing to do with reality.

I chose to use another word for these touches: "hyperbole." I don't think they're farcical. They are high moments in the theater that become kind of crazy. In the army there were all kinds of outrageous things happening all the time. There were explosions. Falling-down walls. Playing with old pieces of German equipment and getting blown through buildings. Things that have nothing to do with life as we know it. These wild things were going on all through the war. Yet there was a kind of tender, yearning, sad thing going through life at the same time.

That's why when I read Tom Heggen's book *[Mister Roberts]*, I thought, "This is it! This is the story of the service because it's a combination of this crazy, wild, fantastic, exaggerated thing with a lonesome thread going through it. These lonesome men, these frustrated, unfulfilled, bored, unled people." Therefore, when I did this show, I got some screwy effects because I thought they were right. When William Wyler saw the show and people were saying, "Gee, you've got too much blown off the side of his leg because if he [Ensign Pulver] had that much blown off he might have lost his kneecap," I asked him, "Do you think that's overdone?"

"Listen," he said. "It's a custard pie scene, isn't it? You can't go too far with those things." At that point the audience was so happy, they wanted to believe so much that you just gave them enough to satisfy this high moment of outrageousness—this long stretch of the imagination that Kabuki is such a master of.

QUESTION: It occurs to me that the Japanese are a very orderly, polite people and that Kabuki is a fine complement to that kind of people. But do you think that our audiences really need that, since we live such outrageous lives ourselves—a kind of national Kabuki existence—anyway? [Laughter.]

MR. LOGAN: The politeness you speak of may exist, but actually there is such a wealth of change—long, orderly passages in Kabuki that are very traditional, based on the much earlier artistic culture of the No theater. A classical theater, like the theater of the Greeks. Theater done with masks.

Faced with the problem of writing plays, we should first solve the problem of our own limitations. I'm fascinated with it. Being held to one set and a time problem makes for wonderful writing, too. I simply think that after a person has done a lot of the same thing, that maybe they might try to do something crazy.

People who try to tell other people who are writing plays what to do are big fat fools. But they keep on doing it because somebody asks them. [Laughter.] Whatever I say tonight you should *not* take into your hearts and believe. You should listen to it and reject it because anybody who gives advice should be like the person who lends money. He should give it and if it isn't accepted, should put it back in his own pocket.

We have a fascinating profession in the theater. But one of the excitements of it is its limitations. Tradition breaking is a very great thing as long as the right tradition is broken. But breaking tradition just to be smart, just to show off, well, that's another thing.

When I was twenty-one, I got this *brilliant* idea of directing, and that was to have two or three of the actors play an entire scene with their backs to the audience. It was two or three years later that I realized that one of the reasons directors don't put people with their backs to the audience was that it had been tried and discarded thousands of years ago. Some way, somehow as a director, I had to find out how to make actors *seem* as though they had their backs to the audience. That way was to never let the audience be conscious of a fourth wall: If I could get the audience so involved in the play that they didn't understand why they always saw the actors' faces because it never occurred to them to wonder. The moment I turned the actors' backs to the audience, I had a proscenium there, because the audience was suddenly conscious of it.

The moment I discovered that, I felt like a light had been turned on in my head. The smart and clever thing was to do the thing that never shocks the audience, that never makes them conscious. Once they are in the dream, once they are under the spell of my story, never make them conscious that they are in a theater until the curtain comes down.

Never bore them, always make it clear, always make it loud enough, make the lights bright enough, get them in the center of the stage. Always cheat the important action so that they can see the actors' eyes. That's the place emotions show almost more than anyplace else.

I once saw a play in which there was a woman who was suspected of having chopped a man to death with a hatchet. The nice young man who was going to marry her daughter suspected her of being a murderess. He was going to describe a chicken being chopped by a hatchet or something. Then he was going to see the way she reacted to that and that was going to tell him whether she was the murderess.

Well, the director was not thinking, "How can I make this thrilling to the audience?" He was trying to make them conscious of what a wonderful director he was by having her back to the audience when the man asked her this question. I said to him, "What do you mean putting her back to the audience? I had waited all evening to see what her eyes were going to look like when the man asked her that!"

He said, "But didn't you see the way she wiggled her foot?" I said, "No. I was trying to see her eyes." He was a bloody fool. He was just playing with the audience to satisfy his own ego.

I was working with Paul Osborne, a brilliant playwright. We worked on *On Borrowed Time* together. He told me he learned something when he was very young. He and another fellow were working together on a play. They were eighteen and writing a play about a boy and a girl. They wrote a scene and its idea was to show that the boy and the girl were in love with one another. They wrote it over and over again and said all kinds of things. But the scene never quite told the fact that the boy and the girl were in love. Finally it was such a problem that they couldn't go on with the rest of the play.

One day Paul said, "Do you suppose I could have him say to the girl, 'I love you'?" They had worked on it six long weeks and then one day they had him say, "I love you," and that solved the play.

Well, it's hard to find better words than that. It's much quicker, saves a lot of rehearsals, and it's also thrilling to hear if it's done correctly and led up to. If you're trying for something different, do it with the story. Or find a fresher way of revealing your characters. Don't bother with the technical side. You waste an awful lot of energy trying to think of ways of knocking the audience over the head with a meat cleaver in the first seconds. If you can get them listening and caring the first two minutes, you've got something.

I saw a play recently by a well-established playwright, in which a woman finished a scene and immediately afterwards there is a blackout for ten seconds. Then a light comes up and you see this woman sitting years before the first scene in another costume, and she's soliloquizing about what's going to happen in her life.

I swear to you! There's a playwright who's won Pulitzer Prizes and Critics Awards. All through this play—it was written as though it were a movie—it was as though he said, "Cut," and they could slice it together when she changed her costume. Well, this is as much a part of playwriting as anything to do with words, dialogue, characterization, or anything else.

The very essence of playwriting is what happens onstage between the time the woman says, "Ah, there's the postman! I'll go out and get the letter from the box," and when she comes back on the stage with the letter. If you can fill up that spot, you're really a helluva playwright. That is the complete essence of it, when you can work out something while something is going on offstage that will keep the audience amused, and that also make them believe that that much time could elapse, say, while somebody goes all the way downtown, gets the letter with the check in it, goes to the bank, and comes back with a hundred dollars. It's got to be done. The great playwright is the one who makes you happy while that's being done. You, as the audience, you sit back and suddenly you know in the first two minutes, or one minute, that you're in the hands of someone who knows his business.

Anybody can write a novel, given enough time and given enough space. It takes a really serious person to write a play, a play that really tells a story neatly and well and leaves an audience in a state of exultation. And the people who write plays in three days, they've written the whole play in memory before they sat down to the typewriter. And those people who think you can write a play and not rewrite it—well, they are just dreamers.

QUESTION: At an earlier stage in your career, didn't you study with Stanislavsky?

MR. LOGAN: Yes, I did.

QUESTION: Well, now you're talking about Kabuki. They seem like two incompatible systems.

MR. LOGAN: Well, they're not. The fundamental thing—storytelling—is in both theaters. You read all the absolute drivel about the Stanislavsky method, the Russian theater and all. But that is the most maligned thing. Stanislavsky had as big and wide a palette as Kabuki. His Moscow Art Theater—and I saw, I imagine, twenty of his plays there, as well as all of the operas he was directing—ranged from the most ridiculous, exaggerated farces to Beaumarchais' play, *The Marriage of Figaro*.

One scene I remember, a page went and hid behind some laundry. And there was more laundry on that stage than there has been in any Chinatown. He ran back and forth in it. And it was as spectacular and beautiful as anything I saw in the Kabuki theater in its way. This was directed by Konstantin Stanislavsky.

It's a little hard for me to convince anybody that Stanislavsky wasn't just a man who is limited to "memory of the emotion" or "emotion of the memory"—or whatever the theory is. That system of his was merely a way of breaking tradition. He was able to teach people a way of nonintellectualizing. The big thing about Stanislavsky was that he went from emotion to emotion, and not mental process to mental process. He never stepped out of an emotion and made a mental process and then went into another emotion. These emotions would dissolve into the next one—anger into a comatose state, or pity would dissolve into hope or ecstasy.

What he taught was a way of stimulation of art, a way of stimulating the artist. It's the way a playwright gets stimulus. When you sit down to your typewriter and you imagine a scene—you pull yourself into the emotion of the moment, it's a kind of a make-believe that you're there. You think subconsciously you're back some place where you were in a similar plight and this feeling comes over you. Well, when you get into that mood, suddenly a word occurs to you that wouldn't occur to you if you worked it out mentally.

When I was writing my play called *Wisteria Trees*, I found words and expressions that I didn't even know I *knew*. Because I got back into early childhood. I started talking to myself in a southern accent. The South was my early background. Funny phrases occurred to me. Funny effeminate things suddenly would be happening. I'd suddenly be Helen Hayes walking around in my room and flutter all over the place and say silly things just because there was something that recalled some of those southern women I knew when I was a little boy. I found funny Negro expressions I didn't remember. I must say, the play was a failure—but all the Southerners liked it. If we'd only toured New Orleans, we might have been able to save the play! [Laughter.]

Today an actor works in New York quite differently than the Russian actor and the Japanese actor. But always there is a similarity in creative art. It has to do with getting into a creative frame of mind. And creation works in strange ways. But the eventual effect of the theater—I'm sure that the Kabuki theater, the Stanislavsky theater, *The King and I*, are all of the same piece, really. They are just in different languages. But the effect is still a story that is told to the listener.

You can simplify playwriting to this: You tell a story. People listen to it. If the story is good, they like it. If the story is bad, they don't like it.

Or if you tell it too long, they don't like it. Or if you tell it too short, they aren't satisfied.

When I was in the army I was taught by what was called a Soldiers' Show Production Team. Five officers came around to various posts and give a demonstration of how to put on Soldiers' shows. They gave an hour on each side of the theater. One hour on direction, one hour on stage lighting, one hour on how to make costumes and makeup, one hour on playwriting, you know, boom, boom, bing! Then we were supposed to go out and do a show. Well, the guy on direction came out and said, "There's two things about direction: Fix it so you can see 'em and so you hear 'em. That's all there is to it." And you know, that's right. Let the playwright do the rest. The director fixes it so that you can see and hear them. But it's hard to do. There's somebody who doesn't talk quite clearly. Or an actor turns his back on the audience or looks down, and you miss the expression on his face because the director didn't stand out there with a BB gun and shoot him every time he did that in rehearsal.

Howard Lindsay uses the phrase "organizing the audience's emotions." What he means is that the audience wants to be told how to feel. They want to be mastered. They want to feel that there's a champion up there and they don't have to worry about it.

I always tell actors, and I think playwrights should feel the same way, you have to dominate them. Tell them, "You lucky people. You got me in charge of you now." Not say, "Gee folks, I hope I can entertain you tonight. I'll be off the stage in just a minute. And, you know, I hope, hope I'm not boring you." They turn against you like horrible beasts! [Laughter.]

When Oscar Hammerstein and I were working on *South Pacific,* every once in a while we'd wonder, "How can we end this scene?" It would be like this: "The captain and the officers walk off and what can happen now?" I say [snaps his fingers], "The island calls him!" Then I shout, "THIS'LL KILL THEM! THE DIRTY BASTARDS. THIS'LL KILL THEM." I'd get so mad at the audience at that moment. I get rid of all the hatred I've had all these years. "I'm gonna get even with 'em! I can just see 'em taking it in! Believing it. Quiet, not coughing." [Laughter throughout.] Oh, it's a thrilling thing!

But it's so hard to master an audience. They're big and strong and there's thousands of them. They form a team the moment the curtain goes up. You never fool them a minute. If somebody says, "I hope the audience didn't notice," you can be sure everybody in the audience noticed. They knew that a line was left out, say, and they were lost for a while. Or they knew the playwright was hoping he could say some sentence real quick so that the audience wouldn't understand the logic of it. But they'd say, "Wait a minute! What the hell is going on? This guy doesn't know what he's doing." Right away. They all say, "Yee . . . ah! [Laughter.] Back to the French Revolution!"

There's a rule they used to quote that you have to tell an audience a thing three times. First you say it in the first scene, then somebody else has to say it, and the third time they believe it. That is just so much junk. If you say it—even half a sentence—the audience says, "Okay, I got it, tell the story. I know who beat him up." [Laughter.] I'm talking about this horrible thing, exposition. Because that's the hardest thing in the world. But the best thing is to cut it out!

In the first scene of *Mister Roberts* we had long lines like "We're in the South Pacific." "Why it's only three thousand miles to New Guinea from here!" And "My, the captain is a horrible old character." Almost as bad as that. Well, one day we looked at the scene and said, "Let's make this the no-exposition of 1949." And we took it all out—everything that even smelled like it was telling the audience something without its coming just naturally from a character. Then we had a scene.

The audience understood everything. We sweated out how we were going to tell them that the captain was an old . . . But we had a man come out, look at the captain's palm tree and spit on it. The audience laughed. They knew the whole plot right then.

The big thing is to keep ahead of them. You better not pause if you're the director or they'll say the line for you. I remember I had some very dramatic pauses at first in *Mister Roberts*. Oh, they were terrific. Especially when the big revelation would come, something they were going to hold back. For instance, the fact that Roberts had given away the bottle of scotch and then suddenly we learn that Pulver had promised the nurse a bottle of scotch. I took a big pause for the line "Because she said she'd come."

"Yes, if . . . if . . . for one thing and one thing only!" Pulver took a deep breath because I thought it was dramatic and a man in the audience said, "Bottle of scotch."

I wanted to kill that guy. I'd put things like this all the way through the show. The guy in the audience got such a big success on that line [laughter] that he went on all through the evening. Every time just before it was said, he said it! And he said it so that fifty or sixty people turned to him [more laughter], and each time the poor actor had to go on and say it [still more laughter], and he didn't think the line was very good by the time this guy had already said it.

I got more and more furious because toward the end of the play he caught every one of them. From the times that Pulver made the firecracker right up to "He's going to throw the palm overboard," said the guy from the audience. And then poor Roberts had to throw the palm overboard.

I was beginning to hate this man like nobody's ever been hated before. Finally there came that awful moment when Roberts is leaving this ship and a man has presented him with a palm tree medal. He says then, "We haven't had our drink yet." The man says, "No, we ain't." And Roberts picked up his glass, looked at the man and then my pal from the audience says, "To the greatest crew in the U.S.A." But at that point there was no line. The actors just raised their glasses and drank. From the back of the theater, I yelled, "I got you that time, you son of a bitch." [Shouting laughter.]

Oh, God! I sure took out those pauses the next night. I don't think the actors took a breath between lines!

It still gets back to telling a story. It doesn't matter whether you're interested in what happens—it matters that they care about what happens. It doesn't matter if they are fascinated by what happens. It matters whether they care. A show opened the other night, *The Shrike*. I haven't read it or seen it. But the audience got so upset by the play that they hissed once. They got so furious they could hardly stand it.

It may be true that a play can be so depressing that people won't go to see it. But I personally can't wait to see the play because I want to get involved in something I care about. I would love to find something that I hate. That was another reason why I loved *Mister Roberts*—there was somebody to hate.

Villains are supposed to be melodramatic, and you can't have that. But if you can hate, that helps you to care. If you have the power to hate, then you care about the person who's under their power. You get on their side. You hear those clichés and they don't mean anything after a while because they've been said to you so many times they're like French verbs. Phrases like "rooting interest," or "I haven't got anybody to root for." Clichés. You say, "That's old-fashioned playwriting. I want to write something with texture and beauty. Rooting interest! How vulgar can you get!"

At that moment you should listen and translate into terms that sound a little bit better to you, that's all. But don't forget it, because when you forget it you have plots that cannot be successful. Then once you've got the caring—when a play begins and ends you care—then the story can go any way you want. It can go on and on till you get to the ending. That's got to be great. It's got to be worth waiting for.

QUESTION: I wonder whether we cared in *Mister Roberts* because you have the captain, or whether there's something in Mr. Roberts himself— the way you set him up and the way we first meet him—that gets us on his side?

MR. LOGAN: We wrote the scene to make you care for him. The captain really had nothing to do with it. There was criticism of our play. They said it had too obvious a plot. It was often described as "Crew meets boy. Boy loses crew. Boy gets crew." It was dismissed as that. In the book, the author, Tom Heggen, told you to care about Mr. Roberts. He just stepped up and said, "This is the hero." He's the kind of fellow that you just follow automatically. You can't tell an audience that, because nobody would care. You've got to do it by getting the idea across of what makes us care for Mr. Roberts. He was good-looking. He was thin. Had his hair. Yet he was upset almost to the point of disease. He had a lack of confidence in himself because he was on this boat rather than out there with the task force where the better people were.

The moment he was that way, he was a human being who was understood by everyone in the audience. Because they all felt something of that themselves—man, woman, and child. Even the men—the heroes— that saw *Mister Roberts* felt sorry for this guy. Because he was upset about something that they knew wasn't worth having.

Suddenly it was a story of all mankind, as far as the audience was concerned. They sat there and said, "This one I like." Then we thought, "Well, how do we keep them liking him?" If he gets too clean or too superior, then you don't like him one bit. We thought about that a long time. Because Roberts was not written in the book at all. He just talked. He didn't say anything special. It's the most beautifully conceived book that just poured out of this genius of a boy.

But turning it into a play wasn't easy. So we began figuring out how we could keep the audience liking him. Finally—suddenly we nearly stood on our heads! He also looked at the nurses in the shower through the spyglass! If he hadn't, I don't think quite as many people would have liked him. I wouldn't have liked him for not doing it either. If you analyze it from a playwright's standpoint, all of it was done as carefully as you would lay bricks. The thought of his looking through that spyglass was put in so that the audience would like him. We thought, otherwise he'd be a hypocrite.

QUESTION: A lot of plays we get now forget about telling a story. They don't build up to anything. Is that true of the scripts you get?

MR. LOGAN: A play's got to have a story. But the story can be the slimmest thing in the world and have as much punch as the most complicated story. *Roberts* is a simple story. But it was told so that all the drama was brought out. Now, as an example of a technical thing in *Roberts*. I used to get very happy with the audience. I'd find them laughing at something and I could say, "Just you wait! You're laughing and it's only a plant in the first act!"

Very few times in my life have I had this experience of getting a huge laugh on the plant, and then later on an enormous scene that built on that plant. It's what they call in the reviews "a block comedy scene." That means a scene with ten or twelve huge laughs all based on this one little plant. Then at the end of the play, telling the whole thing.

Like when Pulver practiced knocking on the captain's door by rapping on a locker. Roberts said to him, "The first day you have guts enough to actually put those marbles in the captain's overhead and then have the guts to knock on his door and say, 'Captain! I put those marbles in there,' that's the day I'll have to look up to you as a man. Okay?" Pulver says, "Okay."

Then Roberts goes out. Pulver brings out the little inside cardboard roll from a roll of toilet paper and says, "What's that look like, Doc?" Doc says, "Just exactly what it is—the inside of a roll of toilet paper—cardboard center of it." He says, "I suppose it don't look like a firecracker." Doc says, "Not a bit like a firecracker." "I suppose that don't look like a fuse." "Nope, that looks like a piece of string."

"Well, you just wait till old Pulver gets through with it." Doc wanders off and Pulver keeps on talking, thinking he's got an audience. "I'm going to get me some of that black powder from the gunner's mate." Then he says, "No, by God, this ain't gonna be no peanut firecracker. I'm gonna get me some of that stuff they use to blow up bridges, that fulminate of mercury stuff. And then, on the night of Doug's birthday, I'm gonna throw it under the old man's bunk. BAM, BAM, BAM."

Then he knocks on the captain's door—the locker—knock, knock, knock. "Captain! This is Ensign Pulver. I just threw that firecracker under your goddamn bunk!" Big roar! But at that moment, we planted the whole firecracker, the block comedy scene later when he came in with the soapsuds. And when they were laughing at the soapsuds, I always got this playwright's pleasure of saying, "Wait till they get to the end—Bang!" Because I also planted the end at the same time. [Laughter.] Oh, I used to walk around in the lobby and think, "Oh, those innocent people! They don't know what's coming!"

Here's another rule I like, but don't always take it: Every line should do five things. If you can't find five things that it's done, then throw it out. Maybe you could settle for four. No less. It can be the plant of a joke. It can also reveal a little character. It can also add a little poetry or beauty. It can be the payoff of a joke. It can also have a little exposition. But it has to have all those things or it can't fit into a play. Just lines don't mean anything.

Don't let the little ones stay in—those smile lines. If you're going for comedy, cutting to the big laughs is very important. It's not worth it to take that much time. It's not fair to an audience. They want to be entertained. If you start showing off, they won't listen.

I'm talking in a cold-blooded way. When I walk out of here, you'll say, "There goes old moneybags Logan." [Laughter.] But I really think this applies to beautiful and tender plays and poetic plays and art plays as well as just plain plays. The well-made play is the play that puts over its point. Really, it pays off at the end, makes it worthwhile to have sat there all evening.

A play should give you more than a short story gives you. It should be more than an incident. It should have a kind of culmination—which means that it has some kind of emotional change or growth toward the end that makes you come out having had an emotional experience.

Let me recommend Maxwell Anderson's book *Off Broadway.* His essay in that book, "The Essence of Tragedy," is very interesting reading. Maxwell Anderson has had lots of success as a playwright and a lot of failure. But I don't know of anybody in all theatrical writing that I've read who has so carefully analyzed the essence of playwriting. I read that piece and say, "Gee, why do I keep forgetting this?"

He began by analyzing hits. He asked, "What makes one play a flop and another play that seems to be written just as well a hit?" And he began to run through his own plays. He discovered that in his plays that were successful, there was an element that wasn't in his other plays. When he looked at flops, he found that that element was not there.

After he made this wonderful discovery, he realized that it had already been made by a man named Aristotle, many, many years before him. Well, he put it down pretty well—much better than I can tell you. I was working with Max on *Knickerbocker Holiday,* the third play I directed on Broadway. He told me this: Toward the end of a play, the leading protagonist, the leading man or woman, must go through an emotional experience. Underline the word *emotional.* He must either make a discovery that is a matter of plot, something he didn't know about his wife or his mother or something, or a discovery about himself. But he must make a discovery that affects him emotionally. He must learn something that so affects him emotionally that it changes the entire course of his life. The story should aim toward this discovery.

To put it simply, the curtain goes up on one man and goes down on a bigger man, on a wiser man, on a different man.

The New Dramatists Alumni Publications Committee

John von Hartz

Born in Baltimore, Maryland, John von Hartz grew up moving around the country—his father was a newspaperman—living primarily in Chicago and New York. After graduating from Middlebury College, he served for two years in the U.S. Army, then was a reporter for the *Berkshire Eagle* in Pittsfield, Massachusetts. He bummed around Europe for two years, where he married his college sweetheart, Katherine Hughes, in Gibraltar.

Returning to New York, von Hartz worked for many years for Time-Life Books, where he researched and wrote articles on a wide variety of subjects—nature, science, art, boating, home repair. He was a freelance writer and is now retired and managing two brownstones purchased in the 1970s, the income from which provides a life of shabby gentility.

Von Hartz has written many plays, full length and short, most of which had readings, workshops, or off-off-Broadway productions. They include *Down on the Farm, Mothers and Daughters* (optioned for Broadway), *A Little Wine with Lunch* (a revue), *Art Play* (read at the Ensemble Studio Theatre Octoberfest), *Streetscapes* (performed at the Primary Stages one-act play festival), and *A Man in the House*. He was playwright in residence at the off-off-Broadway theater The No Smoking Playhouse. His awards for playwriting include grants from the National Endowment of the Arts and the John Simon Guggenheim Memorial Foundation.

Louis C. Adelman

Louis Adelman received his bachelor of fine arts degree from Carnegie Tech and his master's from Hunter College. His TV credits include scripts for CBS, NBC, and Plautus Productions, and he was a play doctor for the off-Broadway musical *Riverwind*. Adelman attended the Acting Studio playwriting seminar under Clifford Odets, and the Lehman Engel BMI workshop. Formerly a playwriting teacher at Marymount Manhattan College, Adelman has published articles on theater practice for the *Dramatists Guild Quarterly*, and more than forty mini-history plays for *Scholastic* magazine. He has been awarded first prize in the National Playwriting Competition (Ed Kook Arts of the Theater Foundation), a grant-in-aid from the National Institute of Arts and Letters, a PEN grant, and a fellowship at the MacDowell Colony. Adelman is a member of the Dramatists Guild.

Adelman's plays include: *The Barrel Organ, Corner of God,* and *Lady, Ride My Shoulder,* all produced at Carnegie Tech. He also wrote *The Tall Green Grass,* which was optioned for off-Broadway; *The Man with the Golden Arm,* an adaptation of Nelson Algren's novel, which was optioned by David Merrick; *Dressed in Clean Clothes,* winner of the National Playwriting Competition; and the manuscripts *The Riverside Drive, Touch Light, Locking Piece,* and *Witnesses; A Warm Afternoon in Nebraska,* which was read at the South Street Theater; *Night Fishing in Beverly Hills,* which was produced on Theater Row; *Body Language,* which was read at the New Dramatists; *Between Engagements,* which was read at Hudson Guild, sponsored by Gene Feist for Roundabout Theatre Company. Adelman's work in progress is titled *The Oyster Bay Umbrella.*

Anna Marie Barlow

Anna Marie Barlow came into the New York theater as an actress in summer stock and on Broadway in *Festival,* with Paul Henried and Betty Field. A scene she wrote to give herself fresh audition material turned into a one-act play, *Ferryboat,* which won first prize in a one-act play contest. Other one-act plays followed: *Limb of Snow, The Meeting, Mr. Biggs, Cruising Speed 500 MPH.* Barlow's plays have been performed at the White Barn, Westport, Theatre de Lys in New York, and in other off-Broadway productions. Her first full-length play, *Cold Christmas,* won a prize and was performed in regional theaters and adapted for television. She wrote the book for the musical *Half Past Wednesday,* which was performed at New York's Orpheum Theatre. *Glory! Hallelujah!* (a Civil War play) opened at the American Conservatory Theater in San Francisco and on *Theatre in America* for the Public Broadcasting System. Barlow coauthored the book for the Broadway musical *Ambassador,* starring Howard Keel and Danielle Darrieux. Her dramatization of Truman Capote's *Other Voices Other Rooms* was produced by the Buffalo Studio Arena Theatre.

Barlow has been awarded three prizes for her plays; a National Endowment for the Arts grant; and a John Golden Playwrights Award. Barlow's work is published in Stanley Richards' *Best Short Plays of 1980,* in *New American Plays,* and by Dramatists Play Service. Barlow was part of the original team on *All My Children* and other prime time television shows. Barlow is a member of the Dramatists Guild and the Actors Studio Playwrights and Directors Unit.

Charles Best

Charles Best was born in Sewanee, Tennessee, but raised and educated in California. He attended public schools in Santa Ana, Modesto, and Berkeley, and earned a bachelor's degree at the University of California at Berkeley.

Best took a job with the Farm Security Administration, the federal agency set up to assist the Dust Bowl refugees in California. John Steinbeck described these characters in his novel *The Grapes of Wrath.* This service was interrupted when the Japanese attack on Pearl Harbor brought the United States into World War II. Thanks to his language skills, Best was selected by the U.S. Navy to learn Japanese—twelve months of reading, writing, and speaking the language. He was then assigned to Washington to translate intercepted radio messages from Japanese ships.

After the war, Best turned his energies to writing. His first play was a comedy about California "groupies," called *John's Following.* Next came a family drama based on a true incident, titled *Gordon Reilly.* Best moved to New York to study playwriting at Columbia University with John Gassner and Theodore Apstein. With Mr. Apstein's help, his play *Gordon Reilly* was produced off-Broadway in 1953 and ran for four months. Later that same year, Best was admitted to New Dramatists. Subsequently he was elected to the organization's board of directors, a position he holds to this day.

Charles Best has written nine full-length plays, divided almost equally between comedies and dramas. He has also held managerial positions with American Management Association and The World Trade Institute, business seminar and conference providers.

Bonnie Bluh

Bonnie Bluh has been a singer, actor, and performer since the age of three. Her books *Woman to Woman; Banana,* which was recently reissued; *The Old Speak Out;* and the acclaimed recent novel *The Eleanor Roosevelt Girls.* Her new novel, *Falling from the Family Tree,* is scheduled for publication in 2003. Bluh's numerous plays include *The Day God Died, A Lifetime Policy,* and *N, My Name is Nicki.* Bluh has acted on television and in movies. Her performance in *Jesus Christ Is Alive* won her the Best Actress award at the New York Short Film Festival in the early 1990s. Her one-woman show *Celebrating Me* has been performed at the Eugene O'Neill Center and other theater spaces both here and abroad.

Bluh has been a guest on more than seventy radio and TV shows; has lectured in the United States and abroad; and has conducted writing seminars in Russia, Sweden, and Israel. She has taught writing and conducted creative drama sessions and improvisational workshops for underprivileged children.

Listed in *Who's Who* and *Contemporary Authors,* Bluh is a member of the Authors Guild, Dramatists Guild, and AFTRA. She has been a book reviewer, an Emmy Award judge, a consultant for the Lincoln Center Repertory Theatre, and a long-time mentor for the Young Writer's Institute. Bluh has lived in cities from coast to coast and in Ireland, Israel, and Spain. The mother of three sons, she presently resides in New York City.

Joel Wyman

Joel Wyman was born, raised, and educated in New York City, and graduated from New York University with a master's degree. After returning from three years of service in the army during World War II, Wyman subsequently turned to the professional theater and worked for the Theatre Guild and Broadway producers Alexander H. Cohen and Arthur Cantor.

Wyman's full-length plays that were produced professionally are *Dinosaur Wharf,* performed at the National Theatre, New York City (now the

Nederlander Theatre), and the Ivy Tower Playhouse, Spring Lake, New Jersey; *The Day of the Lion,* performed at Cleveland Playhouse, Cleveland, Ohio, the Lyceum Theatre, Edinburgh, Scotland, the Grand Theatre, Blackpool, England, the Hippodrome Theatre, Brighton, England, the Ghana Playhouse, Accra, Ghana, and the Juilliard Theatre Center, New York City; *The Jamison Affair,* performed at Bucks County Playhouse, New Hope, Pennsylvania; and *High Road, Low Bridge,* winner of the Forest Roberts Playwrighting Award at Northern Michigan University, where it was staged with a student cast.

Wyman, who works for Playbill, Inc., is a member of the Dramatists Guild and the Association of Theatrical Press Agents and Managers (ATPAM).